BLESSED
MIGUEL PRO

"Blessed are they that suffer persecution for justice' sake: for theirs is the kingdom of heaven."

—Matthew 5:10

Blessed Miguel Agustín Pro Juárez, S.J. (1891-1927) was martyred for the Faith in Mexico.

BLESSED MIGUEL PRO

20TH-CENTURY MEXICAN MARTYR

By
Ann Ball

*"Greater love than this no man hath, that
a man lay down his life for his friends."*
—John 15:13

TAN BOOKS AND PUBLISHERS, INC.
Rockford, Illinois 61105

Library of Congress Catalog Card No. 96-60532

ISBN 0-89555-542-5

Printed and bound in the United States of America.

TAN BOOKS AND PUBLISHERS, INC.
P.O. Box 424
Rockford, Illinois 61105

1996

DEDICATION

This book is lovingly dedicated to my son Raul, my grandchildren Austin, Max, Tori, Michael and "Angelito," and to the youth of America. May the merry Mexican martyr, Miguel Pro, lead them with love and laughter to *"mi Padre Dios."*

CONTENTS

DECLARATION OF OBEDIENCE

In loving obedience to the decrees of several Roman Pontiffs, in particular those of Pope Urban VIII, I declare that I in no way intend to prejudge Holy Mother Church in the matter of Saints, sanctity, miracles and so forth. Final authority in such matters rests with the See of Rome, to whose judgment I willingly submit.

—Ann Ball

AUTHOR'S PREFACE

My interest in the life of Bl. Miguel Pro, S.J., began over 25 years ago when I had barely begun to gather information for a book on modern saints. In my initial research on his life and martyrdom, I was captivated by his happy nature and spirit of joy combined with a deep seriousness of thought, his consuming zeal for souls, his passion for justice, his dedication to obedience and his strong devotion, as well as his sublime heroism.

After Fr. Pro's beatification I wrote a chaplet in his honor, which I had hoped would help his Cause in some way. My bishop, the Most Rev. Joseph A. Fiorenza, issued an Imprimatur for the chaplet and expressed his hope that, by praying it, many would be brought closer to God through the intercession of Bl. Miguel Pro and that they would experience the deep faith and love for Christ the King which motivated and sustained Bl. Miguel in his priestly mission and martyrdom.

I firmly believe in the Communion of Saints as defined by the Catholic Church, and for me Bl. Miguel is a friend, a counselor, a helper and a guide—not just a subject of my writings. Also, like my beloved patron St. John Bosco, he seems to bring forth love and laughter and happy surprises!

After the approval of the chaplet, through a long-time friend I met Carol and Lawrence Le Leux of

ProVision,* who were enthusiastic supporters of Bl. Miguel. About that same time, I located and was able to speak with the current vice postulator of Fr. Pro's Cause, Fr. Fernando Suarez Santoyo, S.J. From that point it seemed as if my merry Mexican martyr was pushing me to help him spread his joy across the United States, where so many Catholics today, especially our youth, are so badly in need of Christian heroes.

A new medal was struck, and the chaplets were produced. I wrote an article about Fr. Pro, which was published in *Our Sunday Visitor*, a national Catholic paper. In the article, I gave the address of ProVision for those who wanted more information. The paper immediately received a flood of letters from all across the United States from people who seemed hungry to know more about this happy martyr.

Although I could locate a number of articles and brief biographies in collected works in English, it seemed that the major biographies of Bl. Miguel were either in other languages or were out of print and difficult to find. In addition, the blessings and support of my bishop and of Fr. Pro's vice postulator, the comments and blessings from Fr. Molinari (Postulator General of the Jesuits) and from Bishop Tamayo (the auxiliary bishop of my diocese) and from Bishop Ramirez of Las Cruces, as

---

*ProVision is a group of people dedicated to the promotion of Fr. Pro's Cause.

well as the requests, support and prayers of the Le Leux's and of so many others, all convinced me that a new work on Fr. Pro was needed.

Before his death Bl. Miguel told some of his friends that he believed that the offering of his life would be accepted and that martyrdom would be his key to Heaven. He then remarked jokingly that if he were allowed this favor, his friends should get their petitions ready, because from Heaven he would deal out favors as if they were a deck of cards.

It is my sincere prayer that this brief retelling of the story of the Mexican "Joker" will help him in some small way to continue his "game" of uniting hearts to the Sacred Heart of Jesus and of gaining souls for *"mi Padre Dios"*—"God my Father"—which was Bl. Miguel's favorite name for Divine Providence.

—Ann Ball

ACKNOWLEDGMENTS

My thanks are gratefully extended to these and other correspondents and friends—friends of mine and of Bl. Miguel:

Rev. Luis Diaz Borrundo, M.Sp.S.

Rev. John Boscoe, C.S.B.

Rev. Jack Broussard, C.S.B.

Rev. Enrique Cardenas, S.J. (R.I.P.), former Vice Postulator

Rev. A. Dragon, S.J. (R.I.P.)

Most Rev. Joseph A. Fiorenza, Bishop of Galveston-Houston

Rev. Richard Flores

Rev. Bill Frankenberger, C.S.B.

Rev. Troy Gately

Rev. Peter Gumpel, S.J.

Margaret Hotze

Lawrence and Carol Le Leux, ProVision

Sister Margaret Mary, M.C.

Rev. Paolo Molinari, S.J., Postulator General of the Jesuits

Rev. Max Murphy, C.S.B.

Jeanne Noxon

Most Rev. Ricardo Ramirez, C.S.B., Bishop of Las Cruces

Rev. Fernando Suarez Santoyo, S.J., Vice Postulator

Rev. Raphael O'Laughlin, C.S.B.

Very Rev. Enrique San Pedro, S.J. (R.I.P.), former Bishop of Brownsville

Most Rev. James T. Tamayo, Auxiliary Bishop of Galveston-Houston

Bea Whitfil

Bro. David Lopez, O.S.F.

Fausto Zelaya, Jr.

Without their help, encouragement and support, and especially their prayers, I could not have told this story. May God and our merry Mexican martyr bless them.

—Ann Ball

INTRODUCTION

This is a book about one man's love of God, how with true Christian joy he worked for the good of souls and how he gave his life in defense of the Catholic Faith.

This is not a book on politics. Study as much as you like, the political situation of Mexico was, and is, complicated. In this brief work there is not space to include a definitive rendering of all the political motivations and actions in Mexico between 1890 and 1940. Other books detail the problems of the Catholic Church in Mexico.* Most Americans can barely comprehend the situation; the fact that these things occurred so close to our own nation astounds many who think of Mexico only as a Catholic country, not as a persecuted one.

Fr. Pro was by no means the only Catholic to give his life for the Faith during the long, dark years of religious persecution in Mexico. Thousands of Catholics—priests, religious and laity—were harassed, tortured, killed or forced to flee their fatherland.

A cause for beatification has been begun for a number of these heroes for the Faith; the heroic

---

*For details on the history of the Catholic Church in Mexico, see *Blood-Drenched Altars*, by Most Rev. Francis C. Kelley and *Mexican Martyrdom*, by Fr. Wilfrid Parsons, S.J. Both books are published by TAN.

exploits of many live on only in the hearts of their families and in the memories of the people of their native regions. Two examples—one from the beginning and one from the end of the active persecution against the Church in Mexico—are briefly mentioned here.

Fr. Mateo Correa

The holy priest who poured the living water over the infant Miguel Pro was Fr. Mateo Correa. Fr. Correa's life was crowned with his execution for refusing to break the seal of the confessional.

One day the elderly Fr. Correa, obediently continuing his ministry to the people in his area, was taking Viaticum to a sick person when he was surprised by a group of soldiers. He consumed the Host in order that it not be desecrated and he was then taken before the military commander, where he was accused of being in league with the Catholic *Libertadores* (a group of men, also known as the *Cristeros*, who advocated force in order to achieve freedom for the Catholic Church).

Fr. Correa was sent to hear the confessions of prisoners before they were executed. When the commander then demanded to know what the prisoners had told the priest in their confessions, the brave confessor refused to say. He was shot on February 6, 1927.

María de la Luz Camacho

When the former governor of Tabasco, Tomas Garrido Canabal, became the Minister of Agriculture in the cabinet of President Cárdenas in December of 1934, he brought to the capital his own personal shock troops, the *Rojinegros* ("Red Blacks"), a well-trained and disciplined semi-military body of young men and women. Garrido, the "Scourge of Tabasco," preached a mixture of socialism and fanatical anti-religion, and he held weekly "Red Saturdays" in which religious articles and books were burned to the accompaniment of dance and song. Houses and churches in the city were raided for the material for the weekly bonfire. Garrido then began to send his troops to the suburbs to hold demonstrations.

On December 30, 1934, about 50 or 60 of the Rojinegros gathered near the church of the Immaculate Conception at Coyoacan. Mass had begun. A group of about 20 lay persons, having been warned that the Rojinegros planned to burn the church, stood on the steps to defend the entrance at least long enough for the children inside to escape. The minutes ticked away. At last the revolutionaries charged forward, shouting, "*¡Viva la Revolución!*"

With her arms outstretched in the form of a cross, the valiant catechist and member of Catholic Action, María de la Luz Camacho, cried out, "*¡Viva Cristo Rey!*" ("Long live Christ the King!"). The pistols spoke, and María and four men fell lifeless on the steps of the church. There was a moment of stunned silence, and then the unarmed crowd leaped at the assassins—who fled, armed though they were, and took refuge in the police station.

The assassins were imprisoned, but Garrido sent them a case of champagne to cheer them up. They were later released; nothing was done to them.

The funeral of María de la Luz and the others was a triumph, with thousands of people attending. After this incident the university students were stirred to the defense and the Rojinegros met opposition wherever they went, until June of that year (1934), when Garrido was forced out of the government in a purge, and he and his troops returned to Tabasco.

Left: Father Mateo Correa, who was executed in 1927 for refusing to break the seal of Confession.
Right: María de la Luz Camacho, who was shot by the Rojinegros in 1934 while defending the entrance of Immaculate Conception Church at Coyoacon.

BLESSED MIGUEL PRO

"And though in the sight of men, they suffered torments, their hope is full of immortality."

—Wisdom 3:4

Chapter 1

A LIVELY CHILDHOOD

There is more adventure, excitement and danger in the life of the Mexican priest Fr. Miguel Pro than in many modern spy thrillers. His life of danger began when, still only a toddler, he managed to escape the watchful eye of his nursemaid and crawl out onto a window ledge three stories above a busy street. There his horrified mother found and rescued him. A final dangerous episode would lead to his death in front of a firing squad at the age of 36.

Miguel was born on January 13, 1891, at Guadalupe, Zacatecas, near the center of one of Mexico's richest silver mining areas. He was the third child and the first son of Don Miguel Pro and his wife Josefa Juárez. Miguel's father, like his father before him, was a mining engineer.

Miguel was baptized three days after his birth in the Franciscan monastery's Nápoles chapel. He was given the lengthy and impressive name José Ramon Miguel Agustín Pro Juárez. His paternal grandparents were his godparents. A family treasure, a small container of water from the Holy Land, was used at the Baptism.

When Miguel was still a baby, the family moved to Mexico City. There, in the family's large and spacious home, Miguel took his first steps. There, too, his investigative impulses and incessant physical activity constantly drew him into mischief.

Through the open windows, the baby listened daily to the hawking cries of the street vendors. One of these vendors, a shy Aztec woman, supplied the family with delicious fruit. This woman became a particular favorite of the young Miguel and often stopped to play with him, calling him her little "soul baby." She began to bring him treats, and one day she brought a large gourd filled with a small fruit called *tojocotes*. Before his family realized what he was up to, Miguel had greedily consumed half the fruit. This caused some type of poisoning, and Miguel became violently ill and congested and seemed in danger of death.

After several days, during which his Aztec friend sat sorrowfully by his bed, anguished at what her gift had wrought and pleading with the Virgin of Guadalupe for the child's life, Miguel's fevers left. Apparently he had also suffered a brain fever, and the small victim was left with the vacuous stare and open mouth of an imbecile.

For a year the baby was sick and could not utter a syllable. A new fever developed, following bouts with measles and whooping cough, and the threat to his life seemed even greater than it had the previous year. Miguel suffered convulsions, and the doctors announced that death was imminent. The family gathered sadly around the child's bed to wait for the end. Suddenly, Don Miguel snatched the insensible form of his son from the crib, and holding the baby out toward an image of Our Lady of Guadalupe, he cried out, "My Mother, give me back my son!"

In the silence that followed, the startled witnesses saw the baby give an immense shudder and vomit a great bloody mass of phlegm at his father. The danger was over.

Within a few days, the baby was restored to full health. He looked at his adoring mother and said, "Mama, I want a cocol" (a variety of roll which had always been his favorite). The happy mother caught Miguel up and hugged him, crying, "Come here, my little cocol!" Years later, when he was hiding from the police, Miguel frequently signed his letters to his fellow Christians with the nickname "Cocol."

From childhood, laughter and high spirits were hallmarks of Miguel's personality. He was constantly in motion, physically and mentally. A born clown, Miguel was blessed with a sunny disposition and a playfulness that enriched the family's nightly gatherings. The five-year-old Miguel would enthusiastically entertain the family by reciting verses, performing charades or directing his sisters in little skits. Seeing his son's talent, Don Miguel presented the little boy with a tiny theater, and Miguel's mother helped him shop for the puppets that he needed to people it. Years later, his dramatic ability remained. A friend remarked that Miguel was a born actor and could laugh one minute and cry the next. He went on to say that Miguel could laugh with one side of his face and cry with the other.

Punishment was rare in the Pro household; instead, Don Miguel encouraged the good behavior of his children with a Saturday ritual whereby some "good angels" brought small gifts to those of the children who had behaved exceptionally well that week. Those omitted from the favors of the "angels" strove to be remembered the following week. Miguel did earn a spanking, however, when at the age of five he threw a minor temper fit in a store while on an outing with his mother and sisters. Later, the very sight of the little white horse which had occasioned the fit was enough to bring tears to his eyes, and he once remarked, "For that thing I made my mother weep!"

Another occasion for discipline came about the day that Miguel destroyed his sisters' dolls. As his excuse, Miguel gave the fact that he was carrying on a "battle"—for which he was dressed in the little general's uniform he had received as a Christmas present—and he had stabbed and beheaded the recalcitrant dolls because they had refused to move. His father replied that, in that case, Miguel's punishment was due to the face that Miguel had moved too much.

When Miguel was six, the family moved to the northern industrial city of Monterrey, where Miguel began formal classes in a private school run by two sisters, the Señoritas Sánchez. For the active little boy, fun and curiosity still took priority. One day he even skipped school in order to see the arrival of the snow-covered trains at the large train station in the city.

Other anecdotes, too, are recorded of Miguel's school years. There was the time he presented a lizard to his teacher as a "gift," the time he "charged" candy at a local store until his mother received the bill and he received his just reward, and the time he and another boy got into a real battle over a new hat that Miguel had worn to school. The other boy had ruined the new hat by pulling it down on Miguel's head, so Miguel jumped in with ready fists. On Miguel's return home, his mother noticed his black eye and asked what had happened. When he told her about the fight, she commented that he seemed to have gotten the worst of it. "Oh, no," he replied, "the other boy has two black eyes!"

In 1889 Don Miguel was transferred from Monterrey back to Zacatecas, where he became the senior engineer at the Concepción del Oro mine. He was concerned by the lack of good schools in the rough mining area, but he did not want to separate his close-knit family. Seven-year-old Miguel and his five brothers and sisters happily packed for what seemed to them only a new adventure.

Housing was also lacking in Zacatecas, so the family lived for a time in the local hotel while a new home was being built. During this time, the protective parents tried to isolate their children from other travelers who were staying in the hotel, and they forbade the children to mingle with them. The inquisitive Miguel, while not failing in obedience, managed to hold hurried conversations with some bullfighters on his way to and from supper at the hotel dining room. Their brilliant costumes excited the lively little boy, who, on his return to the Pro family quarters, would mimic the bullfighters in a pleasing parody for his admiring sisters. Years later, when often evading the vigilance of Calles's spies, Miguel sometimes recounted stories of his narrow escapes using the terms of a bullfighter to enliven the telling.

Chapter 2

FORMATIVE YEARS

On the feast of St. Joseph in 1898, Miguel, along with his older sisters Concepción and María de la Luz, made his First Communion at Concepción del Oro's parish church. The storm of barbarism that lay ahead for the Mexican Catholics had not yet begun; so the gentle pastor, Fr. Mateo Correa, and the small communicant, Miguel Pro, had no intimation that both would one day have their names linked again, the second time being in martyrdom for Christ the King. (Fr. Correa would be martyred during the opening terror of the Calles persecution on February 6, 1927, near the city of Durango.)

Because of the lack of good schools, Don Miguel decided to attend to the children's primary education himself, so he set aside time each night to hear the lessons which were assigned daily. From breakfast until the four o'clock Mexican dinner, the children were expected to work at their lessons. Miguel was no serious student, but he studied with his usual obedience. He quickly learned to read and write very well, and his extraordinary memory allowed him to make successful recitations even in the subjects he did not like. In the evenings,

Miguel began to master the guitar and the mandolin. Eventually, under Miguel's direction, the five oldest Pro children made up a string quintet, which gave much pleasure to the family and to visitors at the Pro home. Miguel also enjoyed poetry, and he often wrote verses as presents to family members on special occasions.

Miguel was so fond of music that whenever a band of musicians passed the house, he would drop what he was doing and run to the door. Once, after Miguel had interrupted his studies for a troupe of these roving minstrels, his father forbade him to leave his books or set foot in the street for such a thing. The obedient but ever mischievous youth held his book in his hand and walked on his knees to the door to enjoy the performance of the next musical travelers.

When Miguel was nearly eight years old, his mother suggested that he and his two older sisters help their father in his office on the Saturday paydays. All three children checked the cash that was disbursed, and the girls also helped by stamping the thumbprints that served as payroll receipts. Miguel carried drinks of water to the men as they stood in the long payroll line, and he sometimes gave them his own cookies and sweets.

Although Don Miguel had at first had qualms about the idea because his workers were often crude and quarrelsome, Doña Josefa's plan worked admirably well. The miners respected the innocence of the children, and the help the children provided was of real assistance to their overworked father. Miguel soon became a particular pet of these workmen, and he told them that he, too, was a miner. His name for himself at this time was *"el barreterillo"* ("the little miner"), and in later life he sometimes referred to himself as *"el pobre barretero"* ("the poor miner"). This is yet another of the nicknames Miguel used in his later correspondence while a priest in hiding.

Josefa Juárez was a good and gentle influence on her son Miguel, who observed her charity to the mine workers. Her respect for the dignity and innate goodness of these rough men was transmitted to all of her children. She had a compassionate heart; she understood the restlessness and poverty of the mine workers. She saw the illnesses caused by poor diet and bad sanitation, and she worked to help alleviate them.

The miners were rough men, obstreperous and prone to drunkenness, but Doña Josefa could not forget them or their families, even while accepting the harsh realities of their lifestyle. Their situation was nothing that Don Miguel could change; he was not an owner. But he tried to make sure they received justice under the law and the prevailing practices, and he gave them as much work as the mine could support. Doña Josefa began to visit the workers' families, taking gifts of food, medicine and clothing, and she often attended the sick herself. On her visits she always took along one or more of her older children. Miguel especially enjoyed these trips with his mother. He called the miners *"mi predilectos"* ("my favorites"). Although he did not know how to cure his nation of its social evils, he understood the Christian duty of making individual sacrifice—with good humor and a loving attitude—for the suffering underprivileged, and he understood the value of working for peace with justice.

Doña Josefa's charity to the sick culminated in her development of the small *Hospital de San José*, which was begun to provide free services to the most poverty-stricken of the miners and their families. She gathered donations and aid, and the hospital opened in 1904. Unfortunately, after only a year and a half of operation, the new town mayor *(Presidente Municipal)* decreed that the hospital was too "exclusive" and must be opened to everyone (not just the poor). He also forbade the patients the right to receive the Last Sacraments at the hospital. The Pro family, naturally, withdrew from this work. Miguel understood his mother's sorrow and tried to comfort her with childlike promises to help "her poor" when he was older.

Chapter 3

YOUNG MANHOOD

As work at the mine increased and the Pro family grew to include eight children, Don Miguel could no longer spare the time to teach his children. A succession of private tutors were hired, until at last Don Miguel decided it was time for his son Miguel to be sent away to school. So at the age of ten Miguel went to live with an uncle in Mexico City, but he soon became ill and had to return home.

The following year, Miguel's parents heard of a new school in Saltillo, a city much closer to home. The school seemed a good one, and Miguel was enrolled as a boarder. As it turned out, the school had an anti-Catholic bias, and Miguel was prohibited from attending Mass. Miguel wrote home about this, but no mention of the problem was made in the letters he received from home.

After several weeks, Miguel rebelled and refused to attend the required Protestant services. As a punishment, the headmaster locked him in a room. One day, the young prisoner saw a family through the window of his "prison" and called them over, begging the woman to write to his parents about the situation. The pious lady, a Catholic, promised to notify his parents immediately. Her letter brought the first news of the situation the Pros had heard. Don Miguel boarded the next train for Saltillo and withdrew his son from the school.

When Miguel was 14, his father resigned his position at the mine and was appointed an agent of the National Department of Commerce, Division of Mines. The workload was so heavy that Miguel went to work in his father's office. There he reviewed all the case histories of the mine litigations and was in charge of the files. Although Miguel did not enjoy paperwork, the exceptional memory of this very young man was an outstanding qualification, and in no time he was able to memorize the complicated legal classifications and file numbers. He also became a proficient typist.

Two years later, Don Miguel sent his family to live in Saltillo so the younger children could attend school. Young Miguel moved to Saltillo also. Don Miguel went home to Saltillo on weekends, taking office work for Miguel and bringing the youth's completed work back to Concepción with him when he returned. Already doing an adult's work for his father's office, Miguel began to take more and more part in the domestic affairs of the family also. He took charge of most of the repairs about the house and helped with the supervision of the youngest of the seven children. He was the godfather to his baby brother Roberto. He escorted his mother and his older sisters whenever they went out.

At Concepción, the young Miguel had begun to be popular among the town's hostesses. Although he disliked dancing and would dance only with one of his sisters, he did write many playful and flattering verses to the young ladies. In Saltillo, the social activity was different; here, the older Pro children took great delight in the early evening *paseo*. Circling round and round the plaza, the girls formed a continuous procession, while the boys circled counterclockwise. They greeted their friends and enjoyed the music. At home, the family shared a warm, closeknit life.

Miguel lost none of his happy nature and spirit of fun when he entered his teenage years. He particularly enjoyed practical jokes, which he often played at the expense of his sisters. Once, while taking a stroll with Concepción, he darted over and knocked at the door of a house they were passing. When the man of the house came to the door, Miguel explained that his sister—and he indicated the horrified Concepción—had noticed a beautiful statue of the Virgin in the man's window and wished to purchase it. The embarrassed girl later told her parents that it was the gaudiest, most hideous statue she had ever seen. Luckily, it was a family treasure and the man refused to part with it.

Another time, Miguel attended a mission in a nearby town with some visiting Jesuits who were friends of his family. He secretly dressed himself in a cassock belonging to one of the missionaries and went out on his own little preaching expedition to the neighboring ranchos. He was accepted as a genuine priest by the simple country folk, who loaded the appealing young Padre with eggs, cigarettes and fresh cheeses. The real priests soon caught up with him, but as he had apparently done a good job of preaching, they did not expose him as a fake. Instead they dragged him back to their quarters, where they relieved him of his hard-earned contributions.

Miguel had his own embarrassing moments, too. On one occasion, he was on the roof trying to catch his sister's escaped canary. As he leaned over the side to request help, a shower of forbidden cigarettes fell from his pocket into the face of his startled father. The excuse he managed to manufacture on the way down from the roof sounded weak to all who heard it.

Chapter 4

MOUNTING POLITICAL TENSIONS

In 1907 trouble was brewing at the mines, and Doña Josefa sent Miguel back to Concepción to stay with his father for a few months before the entire family would return during the vacation. Dutifully, Miguel assisted his father during the day with the piles of paperwork which he had always detested. In the lonely evenings at home, sorely missing the company of his family, the rather unstudious young Miguel decided to learn both English and French. Again, his exceptional memory came into play to help him master these languages.

In September of 1907, when the family was reunited in Concepción, a riot broke out during the Independence fiesta. In the middle of the night, with cries of "Exploiters!" ringing through the air, a mob of drunken miners surrounded the office of the *Agencia de Minería*, intent on destroying the property titles to the mines. Since tension had been escalating for some time, Don Miguel had taken the titles upstairs to the Pros' living quarters. As the mob surrounded the office with angry shouting, Don Miguel prepared to go out and attempt to reason with the miners, but his frightened family persuaded him to stay inside. In order to keep up the family's morale and as a counter-demonstration of his own, Miguel grabbed his guitar and began to loudly sing some of his rowdiest songs.

The crowd moved off for a time but soon returned. While the family prayed, Don Miguel and his sons shoved the dining table against the door and prepared to defend their home. Suddenly, there came the sound of pounding horses' hooves and shooting. The Civil Guard, known as the *Rurales*, had arrived. They literally galloped over the demonstrators. Miguel peered through the shutters horrified and cried out, "Oh, the poor things are being killed like dogs! May God in His mercy pardon all of them!"

Although the Pros were thankful for their deliverance from the riot, they had for a long time deeply sympathized with the poor miners, and they knew that violence was no solution. They all prayed for help from Heaven for the miners as well as for their own family.

At the height of the danger, they had all made vows, which they immediately began to fulfill the next day. Miguel, it seemed, had made a promise larger than he realized: He had promised not to have a special girlfriend (*novia*) for a year. Later, he was heard to say, "Pardon me, Lord, I didn't know what I was doing!"

The Pros were devout Catholics, though there is no record that Miguel was an overly pious child. First Friday Communions, fulfillment of religious obligations, daily recitation of the Rosary for the souls of deceased family members and other practices of the Catholic religion, as well as obedience to his parents and devotion to his family, were simply part of Miguel's life. His faith was a source of consolation, beauty and love. Thus, when Miguel at the age of 17 fell into an unfamiliar taciturnity and a chronic impatience and seemed bored by religion, his entire family was shocked and worried. Fortunately, this moodiness was cured by Miguel's attendance at a Jesuit retreat, and its cause was explained by a humorous mix-up in the mail. Miguel mistakenly mailed to his mother a letter intended for his non-Catholic girlfriend, while the letter intended for his mother was mailed to the señorita in question. Doña Josefa had not even suspected that Miguel had accepted this girl as his *novia*. The mix-up led to a break-up with the girl. Later, Miguel admitted that this romantic entanglement had not been caused by any sincere affection for the girl but by pride, and he had not known how to extricate himself.

When Miguel was 18, he and his two oldest sisters spent a wonderful three-month vacation in Zacatecas, visiting with relatives in Guadalupe, their family's native town. After their return home in February of 1909, the family moved again to Saltillo, because now even the youngest child, Roberto, was of school age. This second two-year period in Saltillo was the closest and happiest of times for the family. Their joy was not marred by

the mounting political tensions and problems of
the country.

¡ *Viva mi Padre Dios* !

When Halley's comet made its dramatic appearance in 1910, Miguel stayed up until three o'clock
in the morning to see it. Indeed, the mischievous
youth woke the neighbors with a serenade so that
they, too, could admire it. The beauty of the comet
caused Miguel to exclaim, "¡*Viva mi Padre Dios*, the
Worker of things so lovely! Just wait, little stars—
or big—until you see how I shall outdo you by leaving my trail across the heavens."

Chapter 5

THREE VOCATIONS

In August of 1910, the second of the Pro daughters, María de la Luz, left home to enter the Sisters of the Good Shepherd at Aguascalientes. Miguel felt one of the deepest sorrows he had ever known. Six months after her departure, the family attended her reception of the habit. While there, his sister Concepción also determined to enter the convent. Upon hearing this news, Miguel threw himself on his bed and sobbed. Later, while walking with Concepción, Miguel begged his sister to tell him what it was that was causing her to leave her loved ones. Concepción answered by telling him that it was the will of God. Still sorrowful, Miguel begged her to pray that he, too, could soon learn the will of God for his own life.

The next day the family attended the First Communion of their little Humberto. At the breakfast afterwards—the last the family would ever share together—an emotional Miguel questioned his sisters, asking whether, since they had pledged their lives to religion, he should not do the same. "If what I am feeling now is a divine vocation," Miguel told his sisters, "that's exactly the way it will turn out!" Before leaving, Miguel asked the Superior of the convent to have the nuns pray for him, that he might know what direction he should take.

At home Miguel fell into a deep depression, becoming reserved and pensive, forgetting his jokes and pranks and displaying none of his happy nature. But by Easter his spirits had improved, and he sent his convent sisters a little book he had composed entitled *De Todo un Poco* (*A Little of Everything*), which was a collection of skits, verses and quips. On the first page was a verse he had written when he was only seven:

> Beneath a green palm
>   A sad coyote sat,
> Whose sighing song said,
>   "Drop down, dates!"

Miguel himself was like the sad little coyote, sitting under the date palm of *mi Padre Dios*, singing for God to drop down the "dates" of wisdom as to his future. In August of that same year Miguel requested his parents' permission to apply for entrance to the Jesuits.

Miguel's reputation as a jokester had preceded him to the seminary, and the superiors wanted to make certain that the young man could take a joke as well as play one.

At his first appointment with the rector, Miguel found the priest reading a newspaper. Miguel stood for a full half hour before the rector put down his paper long enough to suggest that Miguel return the next day as he was quite busy at the moment. The next day the rector was busy writing. Again Miguel stood for a long time before being noticed. With difficulty, Miguel kept himself from losing his composure. At the final interview there was a whole group of Jesuits in the courtyard loudly complaining about all the things wrong with the Society of Jesus. It then dawned on Miguel that this was a test—a test he successfully passed. He entered the Jesuit novitiate at the Hacienda El Llano in Michoacan on August 10, 1911.

Miguel was overwhelmed by the amount of studies required. At 20, he had never completed his secondary education and was poorly prepared. He determine to compensate for what he considered his mediocre intellectual powers by relying on his outstanding memory to struggle through his courses and by working for greater spiritual perfection through prayer. His professors and classmates would tease him and call him "the brother who is convinced God wants him to be a saint," but, as one later admitted, there were "two Pros in one: the one who played and the one who prayed." Fr. Bernardo Portas, S.J., in his *Vida del Padre Pro, S.J.*, says, "He who laughed at all the world, beginning with himself, took the things of God more seriously than some would ever have suspected." Sensitive to criticism and having a tendency to proud flashes of resentment, Miguel had to work hard to achieve humility. On August 15, 1913, he made his vows, becoming a professed member of the Society of Jesus.

Chapter 6

FLIGHT FROM MEXICO

In 1910 a revolution began in Mexico. Reports of the atrocities committed against the Mexican religious in all parts of the country filtered up to the novitiate, which had remained in a relatively quiet backwater. By 1914 the fighting was too close for comfort, and the rector of the seminary prepared for the worst. He packed and hid or buried the best possessions of the novitiate and bought street clothes for the members of the community.

On August 4 a group of armed soldiers broke into the novitiate; after doing a slight amount of damage, they left, vowing to return. Dispersal was imminent. On August 15 the novices began leaving in small groups. By foot and train they made their way to Laredo, Texas, a trip that took longer than a month.

On their way to Laredo, Miguel and his traveling companions stopped first in Zamora, a town gripped in terror because of the conduct of the revolutionaries. Here the revolutionary chief had personally beaten an old priest to prove to his troops that the blood of a priest would not wither his hand. For a few days Miguel and one of his companions undertook the task of bringing food to two of the local priests in hiding and missed capture by a group of *Carrancistas* by only a few seconds. They hid, lying flat in a providential cornfield for more than an hour. The order came to continue on their journey, and in one of his first practical uses of his acting skills, Miguel dressed as a peasant, attending his friends as if he were their servant.

Pancho Villa's victory at Saltillo had resulted in the Pro family's financial ruin and the dispersion of the family members. Don Miguel's previous government service made him a marked man and he was forced to flee for his life. Doña Josefa, Anna María and the three youngest boys escaped to Guadalajara and moved into a single miserable room of a boardinghouse, with only two beds, some chairs and a painting of the Sacred Heart which Josefa had somehow managed to take with her. In spite of her age and poor health, Josefa began doing manual labor in order to provide for the younger children.

On arriving in Guadalajara, Miguel was brokenhearted to see his family's poverty but overwhelmed at the heroic faith of his uncomplaining mother. His worry about his family's situation brought on excruciating headaches and extreme stomach pains. He carefully hid his pain from his family, enlivening both his visits to them and the daily meetings with his Jesuit companions by his jokes, antics and little skits.

After a few brief weeks, Miguel and his companions were ordered to leave for the Jesuit house in Laredo, Texas. Standing on the platform at the train station, Miguel looked into the eyes of his mother for what would be the last time, and their hearts met. Doña Josefa had entrusted the welfare of herself and her youngest children to the mercy of Heaven; she expected her eldest son to do the same.

From Mexico to Texas, to California, to Spain, Nicaragua and Belgium, the young seminarian traveled. At each stop he worked, studied, played and, most of all, prayed.

From Texas to California

The little group of seminarians stayed a few days with the Jesuits in Laredo and then traveled to San Antonio, where they were given a kind welcome by the Oblate Fathers (Religious of the Immaculate Heart of Mary). After a few days of relaxation here, they stopped briefly to visit the Jesuits in El Paso, happy to be able to speak their native language with some of the members before going west.

On October 6, 1914, the exiled Mexican Jesuits arrived in the Jesuit province of California, where they would be stationed in the small town of Los Gatos. As they entered the town, one of the first sights the little group saw was a large statue of the Sacred Heart, which seemed a welcome from a loving Father to His sons. The warm and loving hospitality with which they were met by their

American brothers proved the truth of the initial impression.

The stay in Los Gatos was not a long one. Studying was made difficult by the lack of books in Spanish, and although the Jesuits were offered all the hospitality possible, the housing was crowded. On June 21, 1915, Miguel and 15 companions left, traveling by train across the United States to Florida and then embarking eastward on a ship from Key West. After short stops in Havana, Cuba and New York, they arrived in Cádiz, Spain.

Granada

For the next five years, Miguel continued his studies in Granada. He made heroic attempts to compensate for his poor scholarship by spiritual mastery and determined to accept his sorrows with joy. Worry about his family and his intense physical pain were covered with jokes; he struggled to achieve control of his impulsive nature. One of Miguel's fellow novices said that they could always guess when he had received particularly distressing news from home, or when the pain was worse, because it was precisely then that he was outwardly more jovial.

Miguel's happy nature and his genuine love and concern for his brothers in religion made him one of the most popular members of the community. He was always ready to volunteer for the most menial of tasks, and his humility came across to all as genuine. He particularly could not bear sadness in others. He drew caricatures and sketches, wrote playful epigrams and verses and spent many hours planning and carrying out diversions for his classmates. When things grew dull in the classroom, Miguel was the first to liven them up. The seminarians had little access to the newspapers of Granada, so Miguel made his own newspaper, which he called his "scandal sheet." A special feature of this hand-drawn newspaper was the cartoons, which pictured the great controversies of theology in unusual ways.

In addition to working on his studies, Miguel taught catechism in a number of areas nearby. In particular, he loved working with the gypsies. A tribe of gypsies lived in the hills near Albolete. They were poor and ignorant of religion, but Miguel's friendliness, his interest in their welfare and his humor drew them to him. First the children, then the adults came to have a good time while listening to talks on religious subjects. The women, who did not know their young catechist's name, called him *"Padre Primoroso"* ("Father Delightful," or "Father Enchanting").

Granada de Nicaragua

In 1920 when Miguel had completed his studies in philosophy, his Spanish superiors sent him to the *Colegio* in Granada de Nicaragua, which the Mexican Jesuits had opened when they were first forced into exile. For two years he worked in the hot and humid climate, teaching the younger students and supervising the older ones. He taught catechism to the Colegio's servants and some of the townspeople. In his second year Miguel was made supervisor of the upperclassmen who boarded at the school. Rain, insects, scorpions, snakes and the highjinks of the adolescent students often kept him up most of the night. His students, however, later affirmed that their professor had provided some of their happiest school memories. During vacations, Miguel arranged games for them and entertained them by singing happy songs from his homeland, accompanied by his ever-present guitar.

In July of 1922, Miguel was ordered to return to Sarría, near Barcelona, Spain, to begin his theology studies. Here the pain from his stomach affliction increased, but it seemed as if the increased pain also called forth an increase in sensitivity to the suffering of others. Miguel accepted his poor health as his own private cross and he was careful to conceal it from those around him.

Belgium

In the summer of 1924, Miguel was sent to the school of theology conducted by the Jesuits of the Province of Champagne at Enghien, Belgium. It was here that he also began training as a priest for the working classes. Miguel's background with the mine workers of his youth and his deep interest in labor issues made him a perfect candidate for this type of ministry. His superiors had seen his successes with those who made their living by manual labor and believed Miguel had the common touch which would help to make him a good apostle to the industrial workers. Miguel, for his part, read and reread the encyclicals of Pope Leo XIII, especially *Rerum Novarum*, which expounded the Christian means of achieving justice between classes of men. The inspiring encyclicals of Pope Pius X on labor were also favorites of Miguel, in whom was crystalizing the realization that God's mercy and justice demanded mercy and justice toward one another on the part of men in this imperfect world.

In the large community of over 100 men from 13 different nations, a language problem initially made the cultivation of new friendships difficult. Before long, however, Miguel became known for his good nature and merry disposition.

Chapter 7

A PRIEST AT LAST

Miguel was ordained in Belgium on August 31, 1925. His only sadness was that none of his family members could be there with him. He told one of his newly ordained classmates, "At last we are priests, and that is enough." After the ceremony, the new priests went to the parlor to give the first blessing to their parents. Fr. Pro went to his room, laid out the photographs of his family on the table and blessed them from the bottom of his heart. He said his first Mass that following Sunday. He wrote to one of his classmates, "At first I felt rather embarrassed, but after the Consecration I felt nothing but heavenly peace and joy . . . the only petition I made to our Blessed Lord was that of being useful to souls."

During vacation that year, Fr. Pro visited the coal mines at Charleroi to familiarize himself with the Belgian miners' working conditions and problems and to help prepare himself for his future apostolate to the workers. He also visited factories and foundries. In September he attended a convocation organized by the Catholic Worker Youth in order to understand how the organization worked to extend the Faith among the laborers and the underprivileged. The interest of this Mexican priest was noted by the Belgians, and a number of articles were written about him in their newspaper years after his departure.

Fr. Pro's success in winning the respect and affection of the Belgian workers became almost legendary. His personality was a magnet that drew them to him.

One day he boarded a train, entering a car containing some coal miners. They greeted his pleasant "Hello" with stony silence, hostility reflected on their rough countenances. Attempting to engage the closest man in conversation, Fr. Pro was met with the flat statement in a rude tone, "Father, we are all socialists."

Fr. Pro replied, "Ah, magnificent! I too am a socialist."

The startled man questioned this immediately. Fr. Pro replied that he was a socialist but not exactly like they were, as they did not even know what socialism really was. He then asked one of them to explain what a socialist was. Hesitantly, one of the men replied that the work of a socialist was "to take all the money from the rich." Smiling, Fr. Pro asked him, "When we have all that money in our hands, what arrangements are we supposed to make to protect it from thieves?"

A few of the miners smiled, but the speaker then rudely added what he felt was an even greater threat: "There are also among us some who are communists."

With a wide smile, Fr. Pro conceded, "Good! I am also a communist. Look, it's already one o'clock and some of you are eating. Well, fine, I'm hungry too. Wouldn't you like to divide your lunch with me?"

At that, most of the others began to laugh, but the speaker demanded, "Weren't you afraid to come in here?" Fr. Pro replied that he was certainly not afraid because he was always well armed.

In a tone of real menace the man then demanded to see Miguel's pistol. Fr. Pro immediately reached in his pocket and brought out his crucifix, raising it and saying, "Here is my weapon. With it along, I have no fear of anyone." Sheepishness replaced the arrogance on the faces of the miners, and for the rest of the ride Fr. Pro delivered a small talk on the operation of his "weapon" which was much more effective than a pistol. As the miners left the train at the next stop, one of them pushed a small package into Fr. Pro's hand. The priest was pleased and touched to find it filled with chocolate pastries.

Later, Fr. Pro enjoyed telling this anecdote, saying, "Bravo for my communists who entertained me so well, who fed me and, as you see, certainly didn't kill me."

Chapter 8

CROSSES OF BODY AND SOUL

Miguel successfully concealed the ever-increasing pains in his stomach by making a joke whenever the pain came, giving himself an excuse to hold his sides and make funny faces to cover a grimace of pain. But when he began to suffer from insomnia and the inability to eat for days at a time, his superiors noticed the dramatic change in his physical appearance.

After six months of doctor's visits, diets, medications and sanitarium rest, an operation was ordered. In a short note to a friend, Miguel wrote, "Operation on the 17th. All goes well. It was more than necessary. The entire stomach was just one bleeding ulcer. Therefore, it was quite time they opened me up, trimmed me and cauterized me."

After the operation Miguel was grief-stricken upon receiving news of his mother's death. At first stunned, he spent the night clutching his crucifix and weeping for the one who had been closer to his heart than any other human being. He had an intuition that his saintly mother was already in Heaven, which he mentioned to his fellow religious. "This morning," he told one, "I wished to say Mass for the peace of her soul, but I could not pray for her; from this I'm certain she is already in Heaven." To a friend, Miguel wrote, "Sorrow is not contrary to perfect conformity to the will of God, so I still mourn. . . . she is in Heaven; from thence she sees me, blesses me and takes care of me. However, that does not stop her orphan children from shedding torrents of tears, nor from feeling in their souls a sorrow that only God can measure."

A second operation was ordered and the doctors decided not to risk using an anesthetic. Fr. Pro asked for his Code of Canon Law to read during the operation. He told his nurse that since he had not studied it well in school, where he had spent his time thinking up pranks to play on the teacher instead, he thought that having the book might help him think up "recompenses for the cruel doctor." As it was, although he held the book tightly, his lips could be seen moving in prayer the entire time of the operation.

After this second operation the pain seemed even worse, and any food provoked an agony that felt like a blazing fire. Miguel bore this with serenity and cheerfulness; the nursing sisters who attended him testified later that they had never seen anything to compare with his patience. When his friends stopped in to cheer him up, they stayed to be cheered up by him instead. He joked about his health and told amusing stories. A remark to one of his co-religious gives a hint as to the source of his courage: "I pray almost all day and during most of the night. After this I find myself refreshed."

A third operation mitigated the pain a little, but Fr. Pro's debilitation was now so alarming that his superiors sent him to the Riviera, to a *pension* for sick priests at Hyères. After six weeks in a hospital, Fr. Pro wrote on January 21 to his Provincial in Mexico about his state of health: "On the 17th of December I underwent a stomach operation. All was going well, and I should have gone back home for Christmas, but compressed hemorrhoids put me back to bed for the second time. On the 5th of January I underwent another operation, which caused an acute pain that still persists. This is usually all over in 20 or 25 days—a month at the most—but God has permitted this second operation to complicate the first one. The continual pain makes me unable to keep any nourishment down. As a result, the wound will not heal up and blood flows freely. The convalescence is drawing out, and I am on the verge of losing my year of theology. It is 40 days since the first operation, and the wound is still bleeding. I think something must have gone wrong. . . ."

He wrote again after the third operation: "The doctors found three openings, with the wound they had made on the 5th of January still open and bleeding, so here I am in bed again, dieting and unable to say Mass, with the prospect of bleeding again as soon as they give me the medicine, which is the rule after an operation. God be praised for it all! He knows the reasons for all these setbacks.

I am quite resigned to it, and I kiss the hand that sends me this suffering."

When he was able to resume some of his duties, Fr. Pro insisted on saying the first Mass in order to let the other priests sleep a bit later, saying it was no hardship to get up early, as he could not sleep anyway. Afterwards, he assisted the other priests with their Masses. When the sister complained that he was doing too much, Fr. Pro told her, "I only wish I were able to serve all the Masses that are celebrated."

Fr. Pro's health, however, was not improving, so his Belgian superiors decided to send him back home to Mexico. Perhaps the sight of his home would improve his health; if not, he would at least have the consolation of dying near his loved ones.

It is probable that Fr. Pro's superiors did not realize how severe the Mexican political situation was. For his part, Fr. Pro believed that it was his mission to spend the rest of his life bringing Christ to his countrymen, without counting the cost or worrying about the danger.

Before leaving, Miguel asked for and received permission to visit Lourdes. Counting the day of his visit as one of the happiest of his life, Miguel wrote, "I was at the feet of my Mother and . . . I felt very deeply within myself her blessed presence and action. . . . for me, going to Lourdes meant finding my heavenly Mother, speaking to her, praying to her—and I found her, spoke to her, prayed to her."

Guadalupe, Zacatecas, Mexico, where Miguel Pro was born on January 13, 1891.

Opposite: Miguel as a little boy. The young Miguel often helped his father at the mines and even nicknamed himself *"el bar-reterillo"* ("the little miner"). Years later, as a priest in hiding, he would use the code name *"el pobre barretero"* ("the poor miner").

Above: Musical entertainment in the Pro household. Miguel mastered the guitar and the mandolin. Eventually, under Miguel's direction, the five oldest Pro children made up a string quintet.

The Pro family. Standing (left to right) are Edmundo, Miguel, and Anna María. Seated (left to right) are María de la Concepción (who later became a nun), Roberto, Doña Josefa (the mother), Humberto, Don Miguel (the father) and María de la Luz (who later became a nun).

Jesuit novices. Miguel (lower right) entered the Jesuit novitiate at age 20.

Miguel with some students in Nicaragua. For two years (before he was ordained to the priesthood) Miguel worked in the hot and humid climate, teaching the younger students and supervising the older ones.

The ordination ceremony of August 31, 1925, at which Miguel Pro became a priest.

Father Miguel Pro as a young priest.

Father Pro (left) with another priest at a priests' convalescent home at Hyères, France. Shortly after his ordination, Miguel underwent three serious stomach operations.

Father Pro with his brothers Humberto (left) and Roberto (right). Both brothers were active members of the National League for the Defense of Religious Liberty in Mexico.

Father Pro reading. He read and reread the encyclicals of Pope Leo XIII and Pope St. Pius X on justice for the working classes.

Father Pro in his study.

Chapter 9

RETURN TO MEXICO:
THE CHURCH GOES
UNDERGROUND

Miguel sailed for Mexico aboard the steamship Cuba on June 24, 1926. Knowing that Calles's rabidly anti-Catholic government was constantly deporting priests and religious from Mexico, he wrote of his arrival at Veracruz: "It was by an extraordinary concession of God that I was admitted into my country. . . . They didn't even open my bags in customs." The day after checking in with the Mexican Jesuit Provincial, Fr. Pro became a working priest at Mexico City's Jesuit Church of Guadalupe.

Within 23 days of his arrival, an order suppressing all public worship was issued. Calles, determined to enforce vigorously the anti-religious provisions of the "Constitution of Queretaro," promulgated a new law in July of 1926 which laicized education—removing it from ecclesiastical control—dissolved religious orders, forbade priests to criticize the government or the laws of the country and put all public worship under the supervi-

sion of the secular powers. By this decree the government restricted public worship to the interior
of churches and declared all churches, monaster-
ies, convents and other religious buildings to be
property of the state. The infamous 33 Articles of
this law sufficed to suppress the freedom of every
exercise of Catholic life in Mexico.

A week before this decree was to go into effect,
the Bishops of Mexico bravely issued an official
statement to the Catholics of Mexico. It read in
part:

> Since the conditions imposed render
> impossible the continuation of the sacred min-
> istry, we have decided, after consulting with
> our Most Holy Father, Pius XI, that, from July
> 31 of the present year until we determine oth-
> erwise, all public worship requiring the par-
> ticipation of priests be suspended in all the
> churches of the Republic.
>
> In order that the faithful may continue
> to pray within them, the churches will not be
> closed, though the priests in charge will with-
> draw from them. We leave the churches to
> the care of the faithful, and we are confident
> that they will preserve with all solicitude the
> sanctuaries which they have inherited from
> their ancestors, or which they have, at the
> cost of such sacrifice, erected and consecrated
> to the worship of God.
>
> The life of the Church is that of its

Divine Founder. Thus, beloved children, the Church in Mexico is today delivered up, persecuted, imprisoned, reduced to a state resembling death. But the Mexican Church will also, after a short period, rise again full of life and strength, more vigorous than ever. Hold fast to this hope.

In the few days remaining before the priests withdrew from the churches, the Mexican Catholics flooded to Confession. In his humorous way, Miguel described his confessional as a jubilee: "Having just left the clinic's smooth pillows, my annoying constitution was unaccustomed to the hard bench of the confessional, which I warmed from 5:00 until 11:00 in the mornings and from 3:30 in the afternoons until 8:00. Twice I fainted and had to be carried out. And, simultaneously, there were all the talks." Baptisms, marriages, talks, conferences—all increased the heavy workload.

With the enactment of these anti-Catholic laws, the Church in Mexico, as in the times of the Roman persecutions, was driven underground. With a supernatural stubbornness, the Mexican clergy determined to remain with the souls entrusted to their care, sharing their sorrows and working to alleviate their sufferings and offering the Holy Sacrifice in various locations, as well as comforting and strengthening the people with the Sacraments. In order to serve their flocks, the priests risked imprisonment, torture and execution.

Because he was unknown as a priest, Fr. Pro was able to minister secretly and successfully to the Catholics of several parishes. He wrote to a friend: "I have what I call 'Eucharistic stations' where, fooling the vigilance of the police, I go each day to give Communion, some days to one place, others to another, with an average of 300 Communions daily." On First Fridays the number would increase; once there were over 1,000 communicants.

The Holy See granted the clergy of Mexico unusual privileges during the persecution. Only the essential parts of the Mass had to be said and no vestments had to be worn during the Mass. (Fr. Pro carried with him a small stole which was cut up after his death and given as relics to the faithful.) Any type of bread could be used for the host, and even a common glass could serve as a chalice, provided that the priest broke it after the Holy Sacrifice so that, in respect for the Precious Blood, it would never again be used for ordinary purposes. These exceptions were allowed so that the faithful would not be denied the graces of the Mass and to make it easier to avert suspicion in case of a police raid.

The Pro family had moved to Mexico City, and Miguel lived with them, carrying out his extremely active ministry throughout the city. Under Fr. Pro's direction, a group of 150 youths spread about the city to give conferences and Christian instruction to the faithful. As they became known to the terrible regime, they were imprisoned, exiled or worse.

Torture and execution were not unknown.

Fr. Pro preached to all classes, giving conferences to bring the people consolation and counsel for their daily life. To continue his secret ministry, he would often adopt a disguise so as to blend in with his audience. Dedicated to bringing the Faith to the working man, Fr. Pro would, for instance, dress as a mechanic to give a talk to a group of chauffeurs (cab and bus drivers). After one of these talks, Fr. Pro wrote to the Jesuit Provincial's secretary: "These were some 150 district chauffeurs of the type that affect Texan hats, dangling forelocks and that spit through the teeth—but people of *pro*, even though exteriorly rude and filthy. [Famous for his puns, Fr. Pro uses one here. In Spanish, the word "pro" means "worth"; thus these cab drivers were people of worth and were also Miguel Pro's people.] In speaking to these I proved to my amazement that I hadn't lost the old flow of coarse and resounding words [learned in his youth from the mine workers]. . . . I refrain from describing the solemnity of this conference in the big yard of some very ordinary folk, around which, in my mechanic's costume and with my cap pulled down to my eyebrows, I kept my sympathetic listeners moving. Blessings on the chauffeurs of all the world!"

In the midst of ever-present danger, Fr. Pro went about his work in seeming tranquility. Numerous close calls with disaster are recorded in his lively correspondence. On one occasion Fr. Pro calmly walked past a policeman to give a message about

Mass to someone less than a block from the official. During one narrow escape, Miguel was barely 50 yards ahead of his pursuers. Spying a passing girl, he linked arms with her and whispered, "Help me—I'm a priest." The girl reacted immediately and perfectly, and the police search group passed by the "lovers" without a backward glance.

Fr. Pro raced back and forth across the capital on his brother's bicycle to give Communion, baptize, perform marriages, hear confessions and administer the Last Rites. Dressed as a bit of a rake in flashy attire, wearing a scraggly mustache and with a cigarette dangling from his lips, he would brazenly wave or pass a joking comment to the policemen on the street as he passed by.

In addition to his spiritual tasks, Fr. Pro began a project of social aid to the poor of the city, collecting and distributing food, clothing and other supplies, and locating housing for many. At the time of his death, he was providing the main support for nearly 100 poverty-stricken families.

Of these families Fr. Pro wrote, "They have the bad habit of eating three times a day, and generally with good appetites. They live in houses for which rent must be paid; they wear shoes that wear out and clothes that become adorned with holes, and they know how to get sick and ask for medicine. . . . It is evident that there is not and cannot be enough money at hand for all these requirements. But I impose on doctors whose friendship I enjoy, and on rich people who lend me houses for six or eight months, with stamped receipts for rent. What I regret is that I have no friends among shoemakers or tailors, and so I have to make such calculations as: six pairs of shoes at a dozen pesos cost 72 pesos. And I have only 20 pesos."

To another friend he wrote, "I have plenty of corn at present, thanks to the color of my face, for you cannot imagine what shame I feel to be begging, and begging more. Fortunately, He for whom I do this does not show Himself niggardly. May He be ever blessed."

Chapter 10

THE FIRST ARREST

Miguel's brother Humberto was an active sup-
porter of the League for the Defense of Religious
Liberty and by December 1926 had already fallen
under police suspicion. The League had several sec-
tions, one of which was dedicated to military
action. Its members had declared themselves to be
independent from ecclesiastical authority (which
neither approved nor condemned them). They
called themselves *Cristeros*, or "soldiers of Christ."
Humberto was never allied to any but the civic
and religious activities of the League and testified
to this under oath shortly before his death.

The Mexican Jesuit Provincial had given clear
instructions forbidding participation in any acts of
the Cristeros. Fr. Pro obeyed these orders and more
than once moderated the imprudent zeal of some of
the young Catholics, trying to influence them not
to exact vengeance. He rebuked them, saying, "You
implicate the cause of the Church with your very
words." Roberto, Miguel's youngest sibling, merely
assisted his brothers in their works of charity.

On December 4 the resistance released 600 balloons in the air over Mexico City, which soon

began to drop their cargo of brightly colored religious leaflets. Calles was furious at being made a fool in his own city and ordered an immediate investigation and reprisal. The Pro house was one of the first to be raided; but finding no one at home, the police determined to arrest and jail any man entering the house during the lunch break. Fr. Pro was the only fish caught in the net. He was arrested and thrown into a cell at the military prison along with six other young men. After reading the arrest order, the jailer laughingly suggested the group have Mass, as one of them was a priest. Fr. Pro later wrote a friend regarding the incident: "We all looked one another over from head to toe wondering who might be the unfortunate priest among us." The jailer said, "He's a Miguel Agustín."

Fr. Pro continued his account: "'Hold on!' I cried loudly. 'This Miguel Agustín is I, but I'm going to say Mass just like I'm going to sleep on a mattress tonight! [The prisoners slept on the floor.] And this Pro after the name—that's my family name, Pro, which someone has confused with Pbro. [the abbreviation for "presbitero," which means "priest"].'"

Fr. Pro was released the next day but had to return twice to "declare" about the balloon incident. "It was a farce during which in all sincerity and good conscience I pulled our worthy rulers' legs, using a humorous tone to tell the truth without compromising anyone. And yet, thinking it over, I'm amazed I wasn't shot for one strong statement,"

Fr. Pro wrote. When asked if he would not like to pay a large fine because Calles was so furious about the balloons, Miguel responded that he would not like to pay any fine for two reasons: one, he had no money, and two, even if he had, he would not use it to support the government for fear of living in lifelong remorse for such an action.

This escape was close, but no closer than many other escapes which Fr. Pro made. As in the jail incident, he would often use his wit and ready humor to escape from tight situations.

After Christmas an order was issued for Fr. Pro's arrest, so he went into strict hiding. The police had apparently concluded that Fr. Pro had written the leaflets and that his brothers had distributed them via the colorful balloon messengers. When the reserves came to arrest the Pro brothers, Miguel managed to bribe them with 50 pesos. The family fled to the homes of friends and relatives, bringing with them only what they could carry.

In a letter to his Provincial, Fr. Pro wrote, "I am a recluse confined to a narrow room with no other horizon than a neighboring yard. Since I am prohibited from showing myself, I am studying. In order not to be indolent I am also (behind the scenes) building my granary, filling empty houses with cereals and eatables of all sorts for the families of the young men who are so bravely defending our liberties. I have various people, more or less organized, who act for me in all this. With them as a front, I do the planning from here."

This confinement to a cramped room was stifling for the priest, who would have much preferred to continue his active ministry. Obedience to superiors, however, kept him there. He continued his letter by saying, "Obedience is superior to sacrifices, which is why I haven't budged from where I am. . . . Nevertheless, the people are in dire need of spiritual assistance. Every day I hear of persons who have died without the Sacraments." He continued with a plea to be allowed to resume his ministry, promising to use caution so as not to be caught and pointing out that "The most they can do is kill me, and that only on the day and in the hour that God has appointed."

In this same letter Fr. Pro added a postscript about his improved health: "My health is like bronze. I haven't had a single day in bed. Only very rarely does my stomach remind me that it was operated upon, and these occasions are, in my opinion, merely its final protests after almost eight years of daily pain." It was, therefore, with the belief that he might live a normal, pain-free life that Fr. Pro, in a spirit of self-abnegation, begged his Provincial for permission to make the sacrifice of returning to the immediate aid of his poor Mexican brethren so starved for the Faith.

Chapter 11

WORKS OF MERCY

With joy Miguel received the letter granting him permission to cautiously resume his ministry. He immediately threw himself back into an active ministry, dispensing the Sacraments and spiritual gifts, and providing corporal aid to the poor. This work of charity was a favorite of the happy young man of God, and time and again he refered to Divine Providence and the deep pockets of "*mi Padre Dios.*" "I haven't a centavo, nor do I believe myself able to find one, since now nobody cares to give anything. . . . Each day I feel the direct action of God upon us, for it is only through Him that these poor ones exist. This auxiliary work is my favorite. What? Who gives me the rice, beans, sugar, corn, etc.? I don't know. Or rather, yes, I do know: *mi Padre Dios*—because in an infinite number of cases and without my having asked anyone for anything and right when all had run out, I have received gifts of supplies without knowing who sent them."

Fr. Pro described his ministry of feeding and clothing the poor as a slavery for which he had to "spin like a top," adding that his luck was as good as that of a petty thief. "As a rule," he once stated, "my purse is as dry as Calles's soul, but it isn't worth-while worrying, since the Procurator of Heaven is generous." When there was a surplus, Fr. Pro would donate it to one of several rescue missions, saying, "We work on the principle of not being stingy with God's purse. To store up provisions for more than a month would be to lack confidence in God." Of Divine Providence Miguel wrote, "I see His hand so palpably in everything that I almost, almost fear they won't kill me in these adventures—which would be a disaster for me because I sigh to go to Heaven and start throwing out arpeggios on the guitar with my guardian angel."

People often gave Fr. Pro money, but they equally often donated valuable objects to raffle, which frequently brought four times their worth. One of these objects, a lady's purse, was the source of a humorous anecdote in his correspondence: "Once I was going along with the purse of a señora which was quite cute (the purse, not the señora) and which had been given to me but five minutes before, when I met a much-painted lady." When the lady asked what he had, Fr. Pro responded, "A lady's pocketbook worth 25 pesos, which, seeing that it is for you, I'll sell for 50 pesos and beg you to send the money to [a certain family]." He continued his letter, "With such indirections, we break down the resistance of all."

Although Fr. Pro did not take any credit for the work of gathering provisions for destitute families, he was often seen going down a road doubled over under a heavy sack. Once, on coming home for dinner, he began to wiggle about and scratch himself. When asked what the problem was, he rather sheepishly replied, "Well, I have been carrying about a turkey hen with all its six chicks—alive, of course—and I rather think I must have inherited their mites."

Often Fr. Pro had to find families to adopt the babies that were quite literally thrust upon him. Once he was riding along in a cab, chatting with the driver, when at a brief stop at a crossroad a man slipped a package into the back of the car. When they arrived at their destination, they examined the package and discovered that it contained a baby in a box! Another time Fr. Pro himself went to bring a baby to its foster parents. He later related, "I made the mistake of putting the baby, all wrapped up in a shawl, by my side on the seat of the car. At the first jolt of the vehicle the little one went flying up into the air, and had I not caught it while it was still in the air, I would probably have had to take it to the cemetery! I decided to hold the baby in my arms the rest of the way; I don't need to tell you how damp my clothes were by the time I gave the child over to its foster parents!"

Another of Fr. Pro's favorite charities was the Institute of the Good Shepherd. Here, girls who had gone astray, as well as abandoned children, were given refuge. Both the sisters who staffed the home and the children loved Fr. Pro. For his part, Fr. Pro

Father Pro in disguise. After he returned to Mexico in 1926,
Father Pro took on many disguises in order to minister secretly
to the persecuted Church.

Left: Father Pro dressed as a "dandy" on one of the streets in Mexico City.
Right: Father Pro disguised as a mechanic in order to give a conference to a group of cab and bus drivers.

The cover of a comic book on Father Pro's life which was published about the time of his beatification. The illustration shows him in his secret ministry, riding his brother's bicycle and passing by police who are unaware he is a priest in hiding.

Destitute children of Mexico. The poverty level was so extreme that Father Pro, in addition to carrying out his spiritual duties, had an active ministry providing the poor with food, clothing and shelter.

had a predilection for the penitents, the Magdalens, and he relied on their prayers. "Once they have given up their hearts to God," he would say, "they leave us behind as far as love is concerned." In addition to hearing their confessions and performing his other priestly duties, Fr. Pro often arrived at the Good Shepherd with his arms full of packages, and occasionally he got his father to take sweets or other small treats to the little ones. The Mother Superior wrote of Fr. Pro's last act of charity to the Good Shepherd: "When Fr. Pro was in the prison, which he was to leave only for his martyrdom, he found a way to get someone to bring us the few pesos he still had left. He wrote on the envelope: 'The time has come for you to bestow upon me your true charity.'"

The pressures of Fr. Pro's daily life had gotten worse, and his spiritual ministry now consisted mainly of hearing confessions and attending the dying. He wrote, "The perils in which we live are terrible if seen with the eyes of the body and not with those of the spirit."

Danger was ever present, but even Miguel's written accounts of the risks and perils abound with high spirits. One account tells how one night about 9:30, while leaving a meeting for government workers, he saw two men waiting for him at the street corner. He describes the encounter: "'My son', I said to myself, 'say goodbye to your skin!' But based on the maxim that he who takes the first step takes two, I walked directly up to them and asked for a match to light my cigarette."

The men told Miguel to get one at the store across the street, but as he entered the store they followed him in. Back in the street the men continued to follow him along. Fr. Pro goes on, using colorful Mexican slang: "'My grandmother—on a bicycle!' I told myself, 'This is really it!'"

Fr. Pro then hailed a cab; his pursuers did the same. The pursuit proceeded at a leisurely pace; the driver of Fr. Pro's cab was a Catholic and followed Fr. Pro's instructions exactly as he gave them. While putting his cap in his pocket and shedding his jacket so his white shirt would show, Fr. Pro told the driver to slow down briefly after turning a corner and then continue on away rather rapidly. As the cab slowed down, Fr. Pro jumped out and leaned nonchalantly against a tree where the pursuers could not fail to see him. Seconds later their car passed, so close as almost to scrape him with their fenders. They saw Fr. Pro leaning against the tree but never dreamed this relaxed fellow who was obviously waiting for a bus was their prey. "I turned around," Fr. Pro relates, "but not with the desired bravado, because I was just beginning to feel the blow this leap had given me. 'All right, son, now we are ready for the next time' was my final thought as I started limping home through the streets."

Fr. Pro pointed out that he had little time to write of all the things in his active life and that he longed for the quiet and order of the ordinary work of a Jesuit; and yet, "Here in the midst of the vortex I am amazed by the special aid of God, the very special graces He grants us in such perils, and how His Presence is now more intimately felt when discouragement comes to make our souls smaller. I understand very well—and three times over—the cry of St. Paul, asking God to take him from this earth. But at the same time I feel the truth of the divine reply: 'My grace is sufficient for thee; for strength is made perfect in infirmity.'" (*2 Cor.* 12:9).

Chapter 12

THE DANGER INCREASES

Calles's term as president was a time of unalleviated terror for the Mexican Catholics. Thousands fled the country; those who remained were inflicted with outrageous violence—robbery, torture and slaughter on a nation-wide scale.

The Mexican government was controlled by two men: Calles and General Obregón. Calles followed Obregón as president, but he planned to return the executive power to Obregón in 1928; the two of them would then take turns as president, farcically keeping the terms of the amended constitution which promised no re-election, a provision which had been written in order to avoid the long-term reign of a dictator.

During the first week of October 1927, there were 300 political assassinations, and by the end of the month two of the opposing presidential candidates were both dead.

Meanwhile, on September 16, 1927, Miguel Pro had completed his final theology examination. After 16 years he at last qualified for full membership in the Jesuit order.

Five days later, as Fr. Pro prepared to say Mass for

a community of nuns living in a private house, he asked the sisters to pray that he might be granted the privilege of offering himself as a victim in the cause of the Faith and for the benefit of the priests of Mexico. For this intention, he offered his Mass. One of these sisters later testified that Miguel had said, "I don't know if it could be purely imaginary or if it really happened, but I feel sure that Our Lord has accepted the plan of this offering."

The Jesuit Mexican Provincial, Fr. Carlos Meyer, also affirmed that, although Fr. Pro always took the precautions required of him by obedience, he nevertheless held an unwavering desire for sacrifice and remained fearless while doing all that was possible for God. Moreover, Miguel had frequently asked his brothers in religion for prayers that he might be allowed to sacrifice his life in defense of the Church.

In mid-October Miguel dashed off a few lines to a friend, telling him that the highlight of the week was the gift of a six-month-old baby boy whose parents had abandoned him. Since he was unable to find a home for the boy, the Pro family decided to adopt him themselves. Fr. Pro had been given other children previously, whom he had placed with various families, but this little José de Jesús, a Jaliscan baby, became the immediate delight of the entire family. The Pros welcomed him with open arms and called him "the Chilpayate," a nickname Indian mothers often used for their babies. Fr. Pro wrote, "Doesn't it seem just that we care for the *niño* God gives us when He has protected every one of our houses through these days of mourning and misery?"

The adoption of this baby by the Pro family led to a vicious rumor. Fr. Mayer, Miguel's superior, was certain there was no impropriety, but the attack on a member of his community vexed him, and he remarked to Fr. Pro, "Defend yourself, Father." Miguel replied, "Not if I can help it. For the first time in my life I am sure of not having committed a fault that I'm reproached for! Defend myself and lose the only chance I have had of imitating Jesus Christ, who kept silent when He was judged unjustly? Oh, no!"

Near the end of the month, Fr. Pro wrote a humorous post card from Toluca, a neighboring city, where he had gone for a brief mission, telling of the success of his conference there. In a more serious letter to the same friend written on October 30, Miguel speaks of wishing to travel to even more cities to speak to the people, and he mentions that his health is so good that he has even been able to eat the greasy sausages (*chorizos*) the area is famous for.

On November 13, 1927, a bomb was thrown from an old Essex in an unsuccessful attempt on the life of General Obregón. The Essex was a car that at one time had belonged to Miguel's brother Humberto. Although all the Pro brothers had solid alibis, they became marked men.

On learning of the use of the Essex in the assassination attempt, the Pro family went into strict hiding, with the intention of leaving the country. Within four days, however, they were betrayed to the police by a young boy who feared for his mother's life.

It is unlikely that Fr. Pro, with his desire for martyrdom, would have wanted to become an exile again, but he was under obedience to take every precaution to prolong his life and was morally responsible for his brothers. He therefore set up a plan for escape, and the family was able to change quarters before their residence was raided.

Two of the would-be assassins, Juan Antonino Tirado and Nahum Lamberto Ruiz (who had been wounded in the attempt), were captured at the time of the incident; two others escaped. Another young man was arrested at the same time but was later released by the police when it was realized that he was not part of the group.

The injured prisoner, Ruiz, was the first to be dragged to the home of Obregón for interrogation. When the General saw that Ruiz's head wound had claimed an eye and that he might die at any time, and that furthermore he was bleeding on the carpet, the disgusted General ordered that he be taken to jail. Obregón then left the interrogation to attend the bullfights that afternoon. Tirado, the second captive, though repeatedly tortured and interrogated by the police, simply refused to talk.

Ruiz was taken to the Juárez Hospital, where he lapsed into a coma and later died. Conflicting reports list him as naming the other "plotters," but it is unlikely that he could have done so. Another suspect, Luis Segura Vilchis, a young engineer for the Light and Power Company, was picked up at work. He made no protestations of innocence or objections as he was taken to jail, telling his captors calmly that he would accompany them "with all pleasure."

Chapter 13

CAPTURE!

On the afternoon of November 15, 1927, Miguel, Humberto and Roberto moved into the home of a courageous Mexican woman named María Valdéz, who accepted them knowing full well that Miguel was a priest being hunted by the police. For two days Miguel and his brothers lived in the room provided by the generous woman, and each morning Miguel celebrated Mass there. Penitents sought out the popular priest and were admitted in spite of the danger.

At the Thursday morning Mass, Señora Valdéz had a moving experience, which she relates as follows: "At the moment of the Elevation, I saw [Fr. Pro] seemingly transformed into a white silhouette and plainly raised above the level of the floor. I experienced a great happiness. Later, my servants told me spontaneously that they had observed the same phenomenon and simultaneously had experienced an exceptional consolation."

That evening Fr. Pro told his hostess that in the morning his brothers would be leaving for the United States and that he would leave on the 19th to resume his "business of souls." He then blessed the marriage of a young couple, and afterwards all in the house went to bed.

The Pro brothers slept the sound sleep of exhausted innocence. Calles, meanwhile, was plotting their destruction. The order for their execution had been given, and that night the house was surrounded by a large group of police. On the previous Sunday (November 13) Miguel had written a prayer to Our Lady, offering to share her Calvary. (See Appendix 1 for the complete prayer.) His prayer was about to be answered.

Señora Valdéz awoke at about three in the morning and noticed about 20 soldiers on her patio. Another group of soldiers broke into the house and entered the room where the Pro brothers were sleeping. Awakened, Fr. Pro exhorted his brothers: "Repent of your sins as if in the very presence of God," and gave them sacramental absolution, encouraging them to remember that they were going to give their lives as an offering for the cause of Religion in Mexico and admonishing them to pray that God would accept their sacrifice.

When the inspector asked Señora Valdéz if she realized she had been harboring the bombers, she replied that she had been hiding a saint. Fr. Pro told the soldiers to leave Señora Valdéz in peace, saying that she was innocent of any wrongdoing. Taking with him only his small profession crucifix and a serape that Señora Valdéz pressed on him because he had given his coat to the poor, Fr. Pro blessed the Señora and her servants as he and his brothers were taken away.

For some reason, on the way to the police station the inspector detoured by the house where Anna María was staying. The owner of the house, Señora Josefina Montes de Oca, had been arrested the previous evening. As his last act in relative liberty, Fr. Pro was allowed to call another friend and ask her to come and stay with his sister as he and his brothers were leaving. When the woman told him to stay and she would come and see him, Fr. Pro replied, "No, *hija* [daughter] . . . not until Heaven."

After preliminary questioning at the jail, Humberto was thrown into a cell with Señora Montes de Oca; Miguel and Roberto were put in a cell marked "No. 1." This was a small, dark room, four and a half feet by nine feet, which was damp and unventilated. Their meals were brought to the prison by Anna María, but by the time the brothers received it, the delicious food was cold and had been shredded in the jailer's examination for secret messages. Anna María was not allowed to see her brothers.

Unlike many of the other prisoners, the Pros were neither beaten nor tortured. The unfortunate Tirado had been tortured with cold water and had become ill, so Fr. Pro sent him the serape that Señora Valdéz had given him. The brothers also shared their food with others in the prison who had none. In between the frequent "questionings," the brothers prayed, sang, performed bounding exercises to keep warm and decorated the walls of their cells with their favorite slogans, *"¡Viva Cristo Rey!"* and *"¡Viva la Virgen de Guadalupe!"* At night they would pray the Rosary together and sing. The brothers were innocent of any complicity in the bombing, said so repeatedly, and were sent time and again back to their cells.

Luis Segura Vilchis, of his own volition, calmly confessed to having been the author and director of the plot against Obregón. His statement named Tirado and Ruiz as co-conspirators, as well as a third man, José González. Segura stated that he did not know González's address, nor did he give a description of him. Segura, a forthright young man, had dedicated his life to the Cristero counter-revolution, convinced that only violence would serve to end the violent tyranny in Mexico. José González, the mystery man who was possibly one of the Cristero chiefs, was never apprehended.

Although the Pros may well have known some things about the Cristero organization and activities, there is no shred of evidence connecting any of the Pro brothers with the violent acts of the Cristeros or with the violent sector of the Religious Defense League. Humberto admitted his dedication to the propaganda work of the Religious Defense League but denied having ever participated in any acts or plans of armed resistance.

As for Fr. Pro, he freely admitted being a priest and, upon questioning, gave an explanation for a mysterious letter to Señor "Cocol" (his childhood nickname and one of his code names) which had been found in his room. The letter was signed "Murillo." The writer was a chauffeur who had become alarmed when he read the news of the bombing, since back when Humberto had owned the Essex, this man had been seen driving it on numerous occasions. Fr. Pro had given the chauffeur 70 pesos in order that he might leave the city and return to his home in Guadalajara to avoid unjust suspicion.

General Roberto Cruz, Calles's Chief of Staff, was in charge of the Acta. He believed Segura's account of the plot and did not feel the Pro brothers were implicated. In addition to the lack of any evidence against them, there was also the factor of the Pro brothers' popularity. Cruz told his attorney that he wanted to get out of the Pro connection and that he wanted to turn their case over to the courts.

Calles, however, would not be cheated of his preferred victims. For despite Miguel's solid alibi for the time of the assassination attempt on General Obregón, he was guilty in the eyes of Calles of an even worse crime—he was a Catholic priest. So General Cruz was ordered to have the prisoners shot.

Though none of the legal process had been completed, Cruz did not want to defy Calles. On November 22 Cruz told his attorney that he had been ordered to have the prisoners shot in the police station and that Calles wanted the event to be a "big show." Calles had instructed Cruz to invite representatives from all the government secretariats, the press and photographers.

Shortly after midnight General Cruz went to the jail in the company of several other military police and a group of photographers. One by one the prisoners were taken from their cells and photographed.

When they returned to their cells, Fr. Pro told Roberto to pray for resignation to whatever was coming. He said they should be happy to suffer something for Jesus Christ, and if worse evils, or even the firing squad, lay ahead, they ought to be proud to suffer and die for Christ. He then spent his last night sleeping on the bare floor because he had given his thin mattress to a fellow prisoner. The next morning Fr. Pro told Roberto that he had a presentiment that something was going to happen that day. He then told Roberto to pray for God's grace, which he assured him would be given to them.

Chapter 14

MARTYRDOM

At ten o'clock that morning, the sweater-clad Fr. Pro was the first to be led out of the cells. No due process had been accorded him; he had not even received a trial. Nor was he told of his impending death, though it seems that he sensed something was about to happen.

Fr. Pro's sister had been advised by the maid whom she had sent to deliver her brothers' breakfast that the jail was full of military men. She hurried over there to see what was going on but was left standing outside the gates, which were shut and barred. A man arrived bearing an *amparo*, a restraining order against the execution of the Pro brothers. But despite his loud cries, which must have been heard, he was not admitted.

Fr. Pro walked across the compound with a steady, measured tread, holding his little crucifix in his right hand and his rosary in his left. General Cruz and his entire staff stood at one side of the yard; little knots of photographers, reporters and distinguished guests stood around, waiting.

One of the policemen who had helped to hunt him down, Valentín Quintana, walked up to the priest and with tears in his eyes begged Fr. Pro to forgive him. Miguel put his arm around the shoulders of the shaking man and said, "You have not only my forgiveness but my thanks."

As his last request, Miguel asked to be allowed to pray. He knelt in front of the bullet-pocked walls and fervently prayed for two minutes. After his prayer he kissed his crucifix and stood with his arms outstretched in the form of a cross, rejecting the offered blindfold. Facing the firing squad, Miguel said, "May God have mercy on you. May God bless you. Lord, You know that I am innocent. With all my heart I forgive my enemies." As the gendarmes took aim, in a firm, clear voice, he spoke his last words: "*¡Viva Cristo Rey!*"—"Long live Christ the King!"

The guns were fired; Fr. Pro met his martyrdom calmly and heroically. But the firing squad did not kill the courageous priest. Though mortally wounded, he still breathed. One of the soldiers walked over and fired a bullet into his head, delivering the *coup de grâce*.

One by one the other prisoners were led out to their execution. Luis Segura Vilchis, only 23 years old, walked unfalteringly and, addressing the firing squad, said, "I am ready, gentlemen." Humberto took out a medal as he passed his brother's body, but he remained self-possessed. Tirado was so ill with pneumonia that he was trembling with a fever; the police had ignored his last request, which was to see his mother. A last-minute phone call

from the Argentine minister to Mexico saved the
life of Roberto Pro, who was later exiled to the
United States.

The photographers, who had been invited by the
fanatic Calles, kept their shutters clicking during
the whole process, and for that reason we have a
good photographic record of the martyrdom. However, the stark photographic display of serenity and
heroism soon made the possession of the photographs a crime.

As the bodies were carried by ambulance to the
hospital morgue, Anna María followed behind, riding with a deputy. At the morgue she was joined
by Edmundo and, shortly thereafter, by Don Miguel.
The old father kissed his sons on the forehead and
wiped their faces with his handkerchief. As Anna
María began weeping, her father admonished her
gently, saying, "Is this how you behave in the presence of saints?"

That afternoon the bodies of Miguel and Humberto lay in the house of a friend. Flowers were
banked in every corner and a constant stream of
visitors came to view the bodies and to pray. The
Blessed Sacrament was even exposed on top of the
casket containing the mortal remains of Miguel Pro.
A holy hour was preached, some of the mourners
went to confession and the Rosary was recited
throughout the night.

At about ten o'clock that evening, five or six of
the government police officers came to the door.
At first, Don Miguel thought they had come to

bother the family, but they humbly begged to be allowed to view the bodies. They were admitted and they fell to their knees in front of the coffins, praying respectfully.

Beginning at six o'clock the next morning, crowds again began to stream in to pay their respects to the bodies of the martyrs. Thousands came from all over the city. Many brought crucifixes and rosaries to touch them to the bodies. Although Calles had forbidden any public demonstration, the people acted in open defiance, knowing that there were not enough jails in Mexico to hold all who wished to pay homage to the saintly priest and his martyred brother. The city had never seen so enormous a turnout for a funeral. One estimate gave 10,000 as the number of mourners; another gave 30,000.

As the martyrs' caskets left the house the spontaneous cry went up: "¡Viva Cristo Rey!" Over 500 cars were in the funeral procession, and thousands thronged the streets to throw flowers on the caskets; others threw flowers from the balconies of their houses. The people walked along to the Dolores Cemetery, praying the Rosary and singing in a shower of flowers. It was a triumph!

This is a rare photo of Father Pro in a cassock after his return to Mexico. During the persecution, priests did not wear clerical clothing.

A priest being executed during the years of religious persecution in Mexico. Many of those who did not flee the country had to suffer outrageous violence—robbery, torture and slaughter on a nationwide scale.

The Mexican government during these years was controlled by two men: Plutarco Elías Calles (left) and Alvaro Obrégon (right).

Juan Antonino Tirado (left) and the 23-year-old Luis Segura Vilchis (right), who, along with two other men, attempted to assassinate General Obregón in November of 1927. Although the Pro brothers had no part in this act, Father Pro and two of his brothers were arrested as suspects.

José de León Toral (standing) on trial for the assassination of General Obregón. The assassination took place eight months after the unsuccessful attempt by Tirado and Segura.

The dungeon-like cell where Father Pro was held after his arrest.

A photograph taken of Father Pro shortly after midnight on November 23, 1927, just hours before his execution. Although Father Pro had a solid alibi for the time of the assassination attempt on Obregón, he was "guilty" of an even worse crime— he was a Catholic priest.

Father Pro being led to his execution. On the morning of the execution, a man arrived at the police station bearing a restraining order against the execution of the Pro brothers—but despite his loud cries from outside the barred gates, he was not admitted.

Father Pro kneeling in front of the bullet-pocked walls. Before
his execution he was allowed a moment to pray.

Opposite upper: Father Pro facing the firing squad. After his prayer Father Pro kissed his crucifix and stood with his arms outstretched in the form of a cross, rejecting the offered blindfold.

Opposite lower: The firing squad taking aim. Father Pro pronounces his last words: *"¡Viva Cristo Rey!"*

Above: The moment of impact.

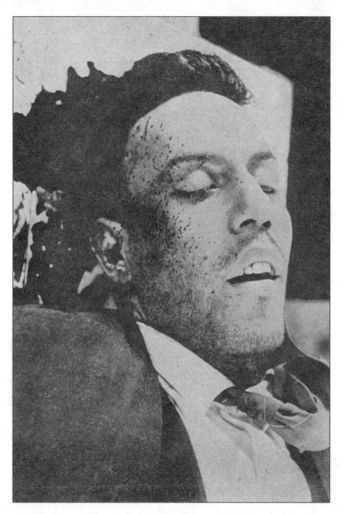

Opposite: A soldier fires a bullet into Father Pro's head, delivering the *coup de grâce*.
Above: Father Miguel Pro in death.

The crowd that stood outside the compound while Father Pro was being executed. The ambulance pictured here carried the body of Father Pro to the hospital morgue.

The funeral procession—which included over 500 cars—passing by the home of President Calles, who had forbidden any public demonstration. The people acted in open defiance, coming by the thousands to pay homage to the saintly Father Pro.

Another scene from the funeral procession.

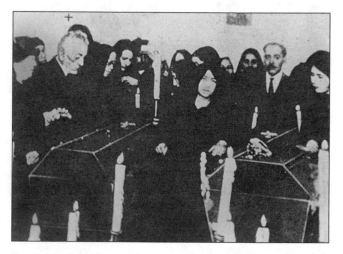

Don Miguel (indicated by a cross) is shown standing by the caskets of his two sons. Father Pro's brother Humberto was executed the same day.

Father Pro's casket is carried by Jesuit priests into the Dolores Cemetery. As the caskets left the house, the spontaneous cry went up: "¡Viva Cristo Rey!"

Father Pro used this stole during his secret ministry in Mexico. It was cut up after his death and the pieces were given to the faithful as relics.

Hago constar que este pequeño fragmento pertenece a la Urna de madera, que durante 30 años, guardó los restos mortales del Beato Miguel Agustín Pro S.J.

Doy fe

P. Fernando Suárez, S.J.
Vicepostulador

Relics of Blessed Miguel Pro. The relic card contains a tiny piece of Father Pro's stole. The wood chips are from the coffin in which his remains rested until his reburial at the time of his beatification. The letter testifies to their authenticity.

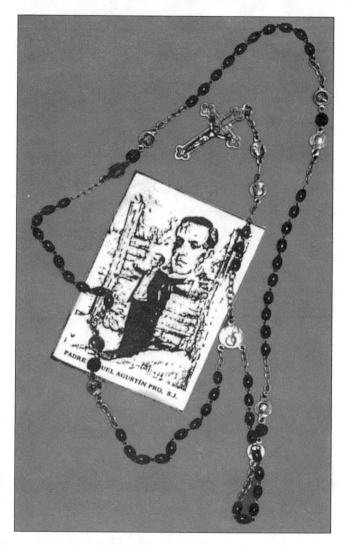

A rosary once owned by Blessed Miguel Pro (believed to be the rosary he held during his execution).

The Blessed Miguel Pro shrine erected by ProVision at St. Francis of Assisi Religious Goods store in Houston, Texas.

Chapter 15

FAVORS FROM HEAVEN

At the entrance to the Dolores Cemetery, the priests who were present asked for the honor of carrying the body of Fr. Pro on their shoulders to the crypt belonging to the Jesuits. Thousands stood by, waving palms and carrying flowers. As the coffin was let down into the crypt, a voice in the crowd began the hymn, "Thou wilt reign, O Jesus," and the multitude picked it up. Don Miguel paid his final respects to the bodies of his sons, and returning to his family, he said, "It is finished. *Te Deum Laudamus* ('We praise Thee, O God')." The priests began to sing the *Te Deum*, and the hearts and lips of others joined in this triumphal song of thanksgiving.

The news of Fr. Pro's death soon spread throughout the world. Calles had wanted the execution to be a spectacle; he did not realize the worldwide reaction it would cause. He gave orders to withdraw the photographs which he had put into circulation, but it was too late. The entire Catholic world had seen how he had murdered the most popular priest in Mexico.

Before his death, Fr. Pro had told a friend, "If I

am ever caught, be prepared to ask me for things when I am in Heaven." (He also jokingly promised to cheer up any long-faced Saints he found in Heaven by performing a gay Mexican hat dance.) Many of his friends and fellow countrymen believed that Fr. Pro would answer their prayers.

Reports of favors granted through Fr. Pro's intercession began to be circulated even before the funeral was over. A poor old woman who had been blind for six years and was therefore unable to leave her suburban town to attend the funeral was persuaded by a friend to ask Fr. Pro's help. As soon as she finished her prayer, she arose full of joy, declaring that she could see. The friend, unable to believe that the woman's prayer could have been answered so quickly, asked her to read a newspaper aloud—which she did without difficulty. The woman and her friend reported the cure to a priest, who then went immediately to Mexico City and informed the Pro family—in the very presence of the coffins of the martyrs.

Earlier that month, a woman who was in financial difficulties had taken some paperwork to Fr. Pro, who promised to help her with advice. After reading about Fr. Pro's death in the newspapers, she went to her lawyer to explain that her advisor had been shot. The astonished attorney then showed her some papers that Fr. Pro had himself delivered to the office only a few minutes before!

Within nine months, other amazing favors were reported. A Poor Clare nun was freed from pain caused by severe internal injuries after applying a relic of Fr. Pro; she was able to rejoin her community in perfect health. A young woman's breast tumors disappeared after asking the martyr's help. A working woman in Spain asked his intercession for her hand, which was to be partly amputated; she was cured without the prescribed operation.

Moved by a wave of spontaneous devotion, in 1934 Rome authorized an examination into a possible Cause for Fr. Pro's beatification. The renown of the martyr was officially recognized by the Church when in 1952 Pope Pius XII signed the decree introduced the Cause.

In that same year the 25th anniversary of Fr. Pro's death was celebrated in Mexico with Masses and with the dedication of a new monument in his honor at the cemetery. A plaque commemorating his martyrdom was placed on the National Lottery Building, which is now located on the site of the *Inspección* where Fr. Pro died. The plaque reads: "On the facing sidewalk, in a line perpendicular to the end of the stairs, died R. P. Miguel Agustín Pro, S.J., shot on 23 November 1927. R.I.P."

Shortly before Fr. Pro's beatification, his remains were translated from the Dolores Cemetery to the Church of the Holy Family in Colonia Roma, a suburb of Mexico City. Here, visitors from all parts of the world come to pray before the tomb of the holy martyr. The inscription over the chapel reads: "In this chapel is venerated the Mexican Fr. Miguel

Augustín Pro, S.J., 1927, model of happiness and fulfillment of duty."

Miguel Agustín Pro Juárez was beatified in Rome by Pope John Paul II on September 25, 1988.

We, too, may call upon this holy martyr, who with his loving, generous and priestly heart gave his life in defense of the Catholic Faith, and who proclaimed with his life, as well as with his death, the reign of Christ the King.

Appendix 1

WRITINGS OF BLESSED MIGUEL PRO

From childhood, Bl. Miguel penned numerous verses and short pieces of prose. As an adult, in addition to his lively and informative correspondence and his reports to the Jesuit Provincial, he wrote letters to penitents and a number of poems and prayers. Some of his little compositions were lively and frivolous; others are among the most beautiful to be found anywhere. The sample of his works below illustrates the loving, courageous and generous heart of this merriest of martyrs who so desired to give souls to God.

On the Feast of Christ the King, 1927, Bl. Miguel begged our Blessed Lord to end the suffering of the Mexican people in this beautiful poem:

Return in Haste, O Lord

O Lord, Thy empty tabernacles mourn
    While we alone upon our Calvary,
As orphans, ask Thee, Jesus, to return
    And dwell again within Thy sanctuary.

Since Thou hast left Thy earthly door ajar,
    Our lovely temples bare and dismal stand;
No chant of choir, no bells resound afar;
    Dread silence hovers o'er our native land.

Since Thou descendest not as Victim meet
    In sacrifice choice graces to bestow,
No roses rill the church with fragrance sweet;
    No lighted candles on the altar glow.

Our naves, once quivering with the mystic flight
    Of prayer that fluttered as a heavenly breath,
Are now as silent as the somber night;
    All seems oblivion, sadness, sleep and death.

O Lord, why has Thy presence from us fled?
    Dost Thou not remember how in days agone
Those countless hearts which in their trials bled
    Found comfort in the light that from Thee shone?

Souls trembling with the thought of morrow's grief,
    Souls crushed beneath the present cross of pain,
Souls tortured by the past—all found relief
    Before the golden door. Oh! come again.

Afflicted, aged, orphan, pilgrim spent
    With teasing struggles on life's darksome way;
The sick and those by cruel hunger bent,
    And sinners burdened—all came here to pray.

To Thee beneath the sacramental veil
   They fondly turned, and ever found relief;
For not a soul, howe'er distressed, could fail
   To draw from Thee sweet solace in its grief.

No grief could stay, no comfort be deferred,
   No trial crush, when Thou wert biding there;
In mystic sweetness still Thy voice was heard,
   Whose accents shattered sin and banished care.

But now no longer dost Thou dwell a King
   Upon our altars, once as bright as day,
And we no more around Thee sweetly sing
   Our anthems. Ah, how long wilt from us stay?

The very breath of Hell floats in the air;
   The cup of crime is filled by tyrant's hand;
And through the hideous gloom no dawning fair
   Of hope is seen to glimmer o'er the land.

The barque of Peter on the stormy sea,
   With Christ, our Leader, wrapt in peaceful sleep,
Seems well-nigh wrecked by man's iniquity,
   That rages like a tempest o'er the deep.

Ah! why dost Thou abandon us, dear Lord?
   A hymn repentant from our hearts we sing.
Thou canst not fail to keep Thy loving word;
   In Mexico the faithful hail Thee King.

Those who offended Thee but yesterday
   Now tear-dimmed eyes turn trustfully to Thee;
With bleeding feet they went a pilgrim's way
   From far and near to plead Thy clemency.

By the bitter tears of those who mourn their dead,
   By our martyrs' blood for Thee shed joyfully,
By crimson stream with which Thy Heart has bled,
   Return in haste to Thy dear sanctuary.

According to one of Fr. Pro's biographers, Rev. M.D. Forrest, M.S.C., the following was composed shortly before his death.

Does our life become from day to day more painful, more oppressive, more replete with afflictions? Blessed be He a thousand times who desires it so. If life be harder, love makes it also stronger, and only this love, grounded on suffering, can carry the Cross of my Lord Jesus Christ. Love without egotism, without relying on self, but enkindling in the depth of the heart an ardent thirst to love and suffer for all those around us: a thirst that neither misfortune nor contempt can extinguish . . .

I believe, O Lord; but strengthen my faith . . . Heart of Jesus, I love Thee; but increase my love. Heart of Jesus, I trust in Thee; but give greater vigor to my confidence. Heart of Jesus, I give my heart to Thee; but so enclose it in Thee that it may never be separated from Thee. Heart of Jesus,

I am all Thine; but take care of my promise so that I may be able to put it in practice even unto the complete sacrifice of my life.

On November 13, 1927, Bl. Miguel wrote a prayer to Our Lady, offering to share her Calvary:

To the Blessed Virgin of Sorrows

Let me live my life at your side, my Mother, and be the companion of your bitter solitude and your profound pain. Let my soul feel your eyes' sad weeping and the abandonment of your heart.

On the road of my life, I do not wish to savor the happiness of Bethlehem, adoring the Child Jesus in your virginal arms. I do not wish to enjoy the amiable presence of Jesus Christ in the humble little house of Nazareth. I do not care to accompany you on your glorious Assumption to the angels' choir.

For my life, I covet the jeers and mockery of Calvary; the slow agony of your Son, the contempt, the ignominy, the infamy of His Cross. I wish to stand at your side, most sorrowful Virgin, strengthening my spirit with your tears, consummating my sacrifice with your martyrdom, sustaining my heart with your solitude, loving my God and your God with the immolation of my being.

Of justice and human rights, Bl. Miguel wrote:

We must speak, cry out against injustice, with confidence and not with fear. We proclaim the principles of the Church, the reign of love, never forgetting that it is sometimes also a reign of justice.

———

Of his love for souls, Bl. Miguel says:

I am ready to give my life for souls, but I want nothing from anyone for myself. All that I want is to lead them to God. If I kept anything for myself, I should be a thief, infamous; I should no longer be a priest.

———

Devoted to the Sacred Heart, Fr. Pro wrote:

In the open heart of Jesus Christ one sees His heart burning with love for you, for me, for all men. . . . But one sees it surrounded with thorns, and in their center, the Cross. This fire of love must light up our poor hearts too, so that it can communicate itself to others—but surrounded with thorns to keep us on our guard against petty self-interests and surmounted by a wide-armed cross to embrace all who surround us and not let us limit our zeal to any particular person.

Appendix 2

PRAYERS

Novena to Blessed Miguel Pro

(Written by Lawrence Le Leux; edited by Margaret Hotze.)

ETERNAL FATHER, You raised up Your heroic servant, Blessed Miguel Pro, as a witness of Your great love and mercy for mankind. He was faithful unto death. When facing his executioners, he forgave them, then stretching out his arms in the sign of the Cross and our Faith, he died proclaiming the name of Your Holy Son.

Let his faithfulness and courage shine before us as an example of true faith in these special times. Let his love of Your Son Jesus and our Blessed Mother Mary be our guide to holiness in our daily lives; and grant us, O Lord, through the intercession of Your martyr priest, Miguel Pro, the favors we now ask (*name your petition or petitions*).

We ask this through Your Son, Jesus Christ, who lives and reigns with You and the Holy Spirit as one true and living God. Amen.

Imprimatur: ✠ Enrique San Pedro, S.J.
Bishop of Brownsville
January 25, 1992

Chaplet of Blessed Miguel Pro
(Composed by the author.)

The chaplet consists of a medal of Bl. Miguel, or a crucifix, followed by six white beads and then eleven red beads.

On the crucifix or medal:

BLESSED MIGUEL, before your death you told your friend to ask you for favors when you were in Heaven. I beg you to intercede for me and, in union with Our Lady and all the Angels and Saints, to ask Our Lord to grant my petition, provided that it be God's Will. (*Here name the request.*)

On the white beads, which symbolize Bl. Miguel Pro's purity:

We honor and adore the triune God.
   Glory be to the Father . . .
We ask the Holy Spirit for guidance.
   Come, Holy Ghost!
We pray as Jesus taught us to pray.
   Our Father . . .

We venerate with love the Virgin Mary.
Hail Mary . . .
All you angels,
bless you the Lord forever.
Saint Joseph, Saint (*name of your patron*), and all
the Saints,
pray for us.

*On the red beads, which symbolize Bl. Miguel Pro's
martyrdom:*

Blessed Miguel, high-spirited youth,
pray for us. Viva Cristo Rey!
Blessed Miguel, loving son and brother,
pray for us. Viva Cristo Rey!
Blessed Miguel, patient novice,
pray for us. Viva Cristo Rey!
Blessed Miguel, exile from your homeland,
pray for us. Viva Cristo Rey!
Blessed Miguel, prayerful religious,
pray for us. Viva Cristo Rey!
Blessed Miguel, sick and suffering,
pray for us. Viva Cristo Rey!
Blessed Miguel, defender of workers,
pray for us. Viva Cristo Rey!
Blessed Miguel, courageous priest in hiding,
pray for us. Viva Cristo Rey!
Blessed Miguel, prisoner in jail,
pray for us. Viva Cristo Rey!
Blessed Miguel, forgiver of persecutors,
pray for us. Viva Cristo Rey!

Blessed Miguel, holy martyr,
pray for us. Viva Cristo Rey!

Imprimatur: ✠ Joseph A. Fiorenza
                Bishop of Galveston-Houston
                August 23, 1995

Prayer for the Canonization Of Blessed Miguel Pro, S.J.

O GOD our Father, Who granted to Your son Miguel Agustín, in his life and in his martyrdom, to seek with enthusiasm Your utmost glory and his own salvation, allow us to follow his example in Your service and to honor You by carrying out our daily duties with fidelity and joy in helping our fellow man. We ask that, if it be Your Will, we may soon honor Blessed Miguel as a new saint of the Church. Through Christ Our Lord. Amen.

Appendix 3

A CELEBRATION IN HONOR OF BLESSED MIGUEL PRO

The feast day of Bl. Miguel Pro is November 23. Families may wish to celebrate by attending Mass together and inviting friends to their home for a family fiesta afterward, in honor of our merry Mexican martyr.

To add a Mexican flavor to the celebration, use brightly colored table decorations. Display a picture of Bl. Miguel as a centerpiece. Serve plenty of good food, play music if you like, and enjoy the companionship and laughter of friends and family. As St. John Bosco said, "Have as much fun as you like, if only you keep from sin."

The following is a recipe for cocol, Bl. Miguel's favorite sweet bread and the source of his childhood nickname. Serve it with Mexican cocoa, lemonade or coffee. As you eat this sweet bread, may it remind you of the spiritual sweetness of the Living Bread, the Eucharistic Christ. And as you gather with family and friends, may you be reminded that you are part of the family of Christ our King.

Cocol*

4 c. flour
1 pkg. active dry yeast
1 c. anise tea
$^1/_4$ c. sugar + 1 tsp. sugar
$^1/_4$ c. butter, margarine or shortening
1 tsp. salt (or less, if preferred)
2 eggs + 1 egg yolk
poppy seeds

Prepare the anise tea by boiling $1^1/_2$ c. water and 3 tsp. anise seeds. Boil for a few minutes and strain out the seeds. (Or, you can leave the seeds in if you like.) Measure out one cup of tea, and add the shortening, salt and $^1/_4$ c. of sugar to the tea.

In a large bowl, combine 2 cups of the flour and the yeast. When tea mixture is lukewarm, add to the flour/yeast.

Add eggs. Beat well. Stir in remaining flour and knead to make a stiff dough. Turn out onto a lightly floured surface and knead until smooth—about ten minutes.

Shape dough into a ball. Place in greased bowl, turning once to grease the surface of dough. Cover and let rise for one hour.

Punch down. Divide dough into 10 or 15 pieces and shape each into a small ball. On lightly floured surface, roll or pat each piece into a circle about

*Our recipe is adapted from a traditional recipe for semita.

three inches in diameter. Place 2 inches apart on a greased baking sheet. Cover and let rise for 30 minutes. With a fork, beat 1 tsp. sugar and 1 egg yolk. Brush the top of each cocol and sprinkle with poppy seeds. Bake at 375° for 18 minutes.

SELECTED BIBLIOGRAPHY

Azuela, Rev. Fernando, S.J. *El Padre Pro: Martir de Cristo Rey, Martir de los Derechos Humanos*. Mexico, 1988.

Ball, Ann. *Modern Saints: Their Lives and Faces, Book I*. Rockford, Ill.: TAN, 1983.

Ball, Ann. *The Persecuted Church*. Avon, New Jersey: Magnificat Press, 1990.

Dragon, Rev. A., S.J. *Father Pro*. Translated by Sister Mary Agnes Chevalier, F.M.I. Mexico City: Buena Prensa, 1959.

———. *Le Père Pro*. Montreal: Les Editions de L'Atelier, 1958.

Forrest, Rev. M.D., M.S.C. *The Life of Father Pro*. St. Paul, Minn.: Radio Replies Press, 1945.

Guinea, Rev. Wilfredo, S.J., ed. *El Padre Pro*. Mexico City: Buena Prensa - Vidas Ejemplares, Vol. II, #19, January 1988.

Hanley, Rev. Boniface, O.F.M. *No Strangers to Violence, No Strangers to Love*. Notre Dame, Ind.: Ave Maria Press, 1983.

Johnson, William Weber, ed. *Mexico*. New York: Time Inc., 1961.

Kelley, Most Rev. Francis Clement. *Blood Drenched Altars—A Catholic Commentary on the History of Mexico*. Milwaukee: Bruce, 1935 (originally subtitled *Mexican Study and Comment*); Rockford, Ill.: TAN, 1987.

Knowles, Leo. *Candidates for Sainthood*. St. Paul, Minn.: Carillon Books, 1978.

Marmoiton, Victor. *Le Père Pro: Apôtre et Martyr*.

Toulouse, France, 1953.

Norman, Mrs. George. *God's Jester*. New York: Benziger Brothers, 1930.

Parsons, Wilfrid, S.J. *Mexican Martyrdom*. New York: Macmillan, 1936; Rockford, Ill.: TAN, 1987.

Quintiliani, Patricia S. *My Treasury of Chaplets*. Worcester, Mass.: Quintiliani, 1995.

Roberto, Brother., C.S.C. *Dawn Brings Glory*. Notre Dame, Ind.: Dujarie Press, 1956.

Royer, Fanchón. *Padre Pro*. New York: P. J. Kenedy & Sons, 1954.

———. *Sanguis Martyrum Semen; Galeria de Martires Mexicanos, Narraciones Veridicas*. San Antonio: Imprenta Universal, undated.

Various pamphlet-type materials from the Cause.

*The Amazing Story of
Catholic Mexico . . .*

BLOOD-DRENCHED ALTARS
A Catholic Commentary On the History of Mexico
by Most Rev. Francis C. Kelley

No. 1054. 502 Pp. PB.
ISBN-3198

20.00

Shows how Catholic Spain, in 300 years, ended Aztec human sacrifice and cannibalism in Mexico, raised the Indians to equality and prosperity, and built a rich Catholic civilization—which was all destroyed by the Great Masonic Revolution (1810-present). Explains the tragedy that is Mexico—where abject poverty and an anti-Catholic government rule in a land rich in resources and still 97% Catholic! Shows why Mexicans are still pouring into the U.S. and supplies the key to understanding this still potentially great land.

MEXICAN MARTYRDOM
by Fr. Wilfrid Parsons, S.J.

No. 1066. 304 Pp. PB.
ISBN-3309

8.50

True stories told to Fr. Parsons or witnessed by him of the persecution of the Catholic Church in Mexico from 1924-1928, when some 2,000 Catholics including 50 priests were put to death under Calles, including Fr. Miguel Pro. An inspiring witness to Catholic fortitude. Proves that hatred for the Catholic Church exists even in our times and can still flare into open and bloody persecution in this our so-called enlightened 20th century.

If you have enjoyed this book, consider making your next selection from among the following . . .

Miraculous Images of Our Lady. *Joan Carroll Cruz.* 20.00
Miraculous Images of Our Lord. *Joan Carroll Cruz.* 13.50
Life of St. Benedict. *St. Gregory the Great.* 1.50
Melanie/Story of La Salette. *Mary Alice Dennis.* 9.00
Douay-Rheims Bible. *Leatherbound.* 35.00
Textual Concordance of Holy Scriptures. HB. *Williams.* 35.00
Confession of a Roman Catholic. *Paul Whitcomb.* 1.25
The Catholic Church Has the Answer. *Paul Whitcomb* 1.25
Ven. Francisco Marto of Fatima. *Cirrincione (comp.)* 1.50
Ven. Jacinta Marto of Fatima. *Cirrincione.* 1.50
Moments Divine—Before Bl. Sacrament. *Reuter.* 8.50
Eucharistic Miracles. *Joan Carroll Cruz.* 15.00
Angels—Cath. Teaching on Angels. *Fr. Pascal Parente.* 7.50
St. Antony of the Desert. *St. Athanasius.* 5.00
The Catechism Explained. *Spirago/Clark.* 37.50
Fourteen Holy Helpers. *Fr. Bonaventure Hammer.* 5.00
The Incorruptibles. *Joan Carroll Cruz.* 13.50
Freemasonry—Mankind's Hidden Enemy. *Bro. C. Madden.* . . 5.00
Guidance to Heaven. *Cardinal Giovanni Bona.* 7.50
Hail Holy Queen! *St. Alphonsus.* 8.00
Lives of the Saints. *Fr. Alban Butler* 18.00
Secular Saints. HB. *Joan Carroll Cruz* 40.00
True Devotion to Mary. *St. Louis De Montfort* 7.00
Saints and Our Children. *Mary Reed Newland.* 12.50
The Sinner's Guide. *Ven. Louis of Granada* 12.00
Sermons of the Curé of Ars. *St. John Vianney.* 12.50
Great Encyclical Letters of Pope Leo XIII 21.00
Soul Sanctified. *Anonymous.* 9.00
Novena of Holy Communions. *Fr. Lawrence Lovasik.* 1.50
St. Thomas Aquinas. *Anonymous* 1.25
Thoughts and Sayings of St. Margaret Mary. 5.00
The 12 Steps to Holiness and Salvation. *St. Alphonsus.* 7.50
St. Therese, The Little Flower. *John Beevers* 6.00
Life of the Blessed Virgin Mary. *Emmerich* 15.00
Padre Pio—The Stigmatist. *Fr. Charles M. Carty* 15.00
Secret of the Rosary. *St. Louis De Montfort.* 3.00
Prayers and Heavenly Promises. *Joan Carroll Cruz.* 5.00
All About the Angels. *Fr. Paul O'Sullivan.* 5.00
Purgatory Explained. (pocket, unabr.). *Fr. Schouppe.* 9.00
Trustful Surrender to Divine Providence. *Bl. Claude.* 4.50
Mystical City of God—Abridged. *Ven. Mary of Agreda* 18.50

Modern Saints—Their Lives & Faces, Bk. 1. *Ann Ball.* 18.00
Modern Saints—Their Lives & Faces, Bk. 2. *Ann Ball.* 20.00
Spiritual Combat. *Dom Lorenzo Scupoli.* 9.00
Christ the King, Lord of History. *Anne Carroll.* 20.00
St. Philomena/Wonder-Worker. *Fr. Paul O'Sullivan.* 6.00
Blessed Eucharist. pocket. *Fr. Mueller.* 9.00
Way of Divine Love. *Sr. Josefa Menendez.* 8.50
Catholic Home Schooling. *Mary Kay Clark* 15.00
Bible History. *Ignatius Schuster.* 10.00
Revelations of St. Bridget 3.00
Where We Got the Bible. *Rev. Henry G. Graham* 6.00
Secret of Confession. *Fr. Paul O'Sullivan* 5.00
Life of Mary/Seen by Mystics. *Raphael Brown (comp.)* 12.50
Story of a Family: Home of St. Therese. *Fr. Piat* 18.50
Thoughts of St. Therese. 6.00
St. Rita of Cascia. *Fr. Joseph Sicardo.* 7.00
St. Anthony the Wonder-Worker. *Charles W. Stoddard* 5.00
Divine Favors Granted to St. Joseph. *Père Binet.* 5.00
The Four Last Things. *Fr. M. von Cochem.* 7.00
Radio Replies. 3 Vols. *Frs. Rumble and Carty* 36.00
Easy Way to Become a Saint. *Fr. Paul O'Sullivan.* 5.00
Prophecy for Today. *Edward Connor.* 5.50
How to be Happy, How to be Holy. *Fr. Paul O'Sullivan.* . . . 7.50
St. Philomena—Powerful with God. *Sr. Marie Helene Mohr.* . 7.00
Introduction to the Devout Life—Unabrgd. *De Sales.* 9.00
Baltimore Catechism No. 1. . . . . 3.00
Baltimore Catechism No. 2. . . . . 4.00
Baltimore Catechism No. 3. . . . . 7.00
Little Catechism of the Curé of Ars 6.00
Dolorous Passion. *Anne Catherine Emmerich* 15.00
Saints Who Saw Mary. *Raphael Brown.* 10.00
Therese Neumann. *Adalbert Vogl.* 13.00
Prayerbook of Favorite Litanies. *Fr. Albert Hebert* 10.00
Liberalism Is a Sin. *Fr. Felix Sarda y Salvany* 7.50
Hell Plus How to Avoid Hell. *Schouppe/Nelson* 10.00
The Wonder of Guadalupe. *Francis Johnston.* 7.50
Imitation of Christ. *Thomas à Kempis.* 9.00
College Apologetics. *Fr. Anthony Alexander.* 12.50
Patron Saint of 1st Communicants. (Age 10 & up). *Windeatt.* 4.00
Miraculous Medal. (Age 10 & up). *Windeatt* 5.00
Little Flower. (Age 10 & up). *Windeatt* 7.00

—*Available through your local Bookdealer—*
Or order direct from the Publisher: 800-437-5876.

Prices guaranteed through December 31, 1997.

ABOUT THE AUTHOR

Ann Ball is a former schoolteacher and is the owner of a private security contracting firm in Houston, Texas. She studied journalism at the University of Texas at Austin and holds a bachelor's degree in education from the University of Houston. Her favorite hobby is writing. She writes poetry for her friends and family, edits a statewide security newspaper and pens articles and features for the Catholic press. She also writes books on the lives of the Saints and the history and customs of the Catholic Faith. Among her best-selling books are *Modern Saints: Their Lives and Faces*—Books One and Two.

Ann Ball has three children, a daughter-in-law and four grandchildren. She resides in Houston with one of her sons, three siamese cats and an antique bathtub full of goldfish.